KB233972

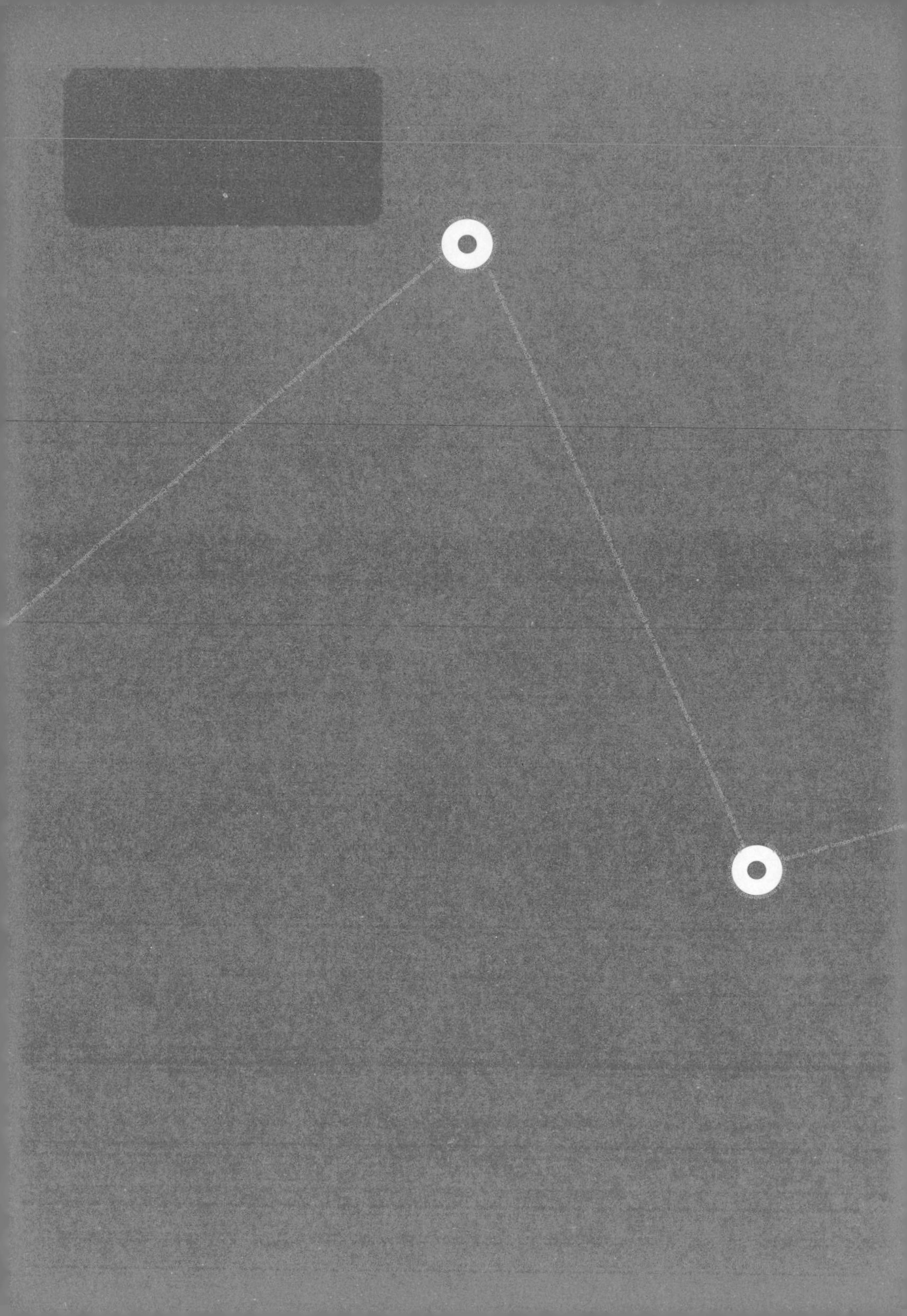

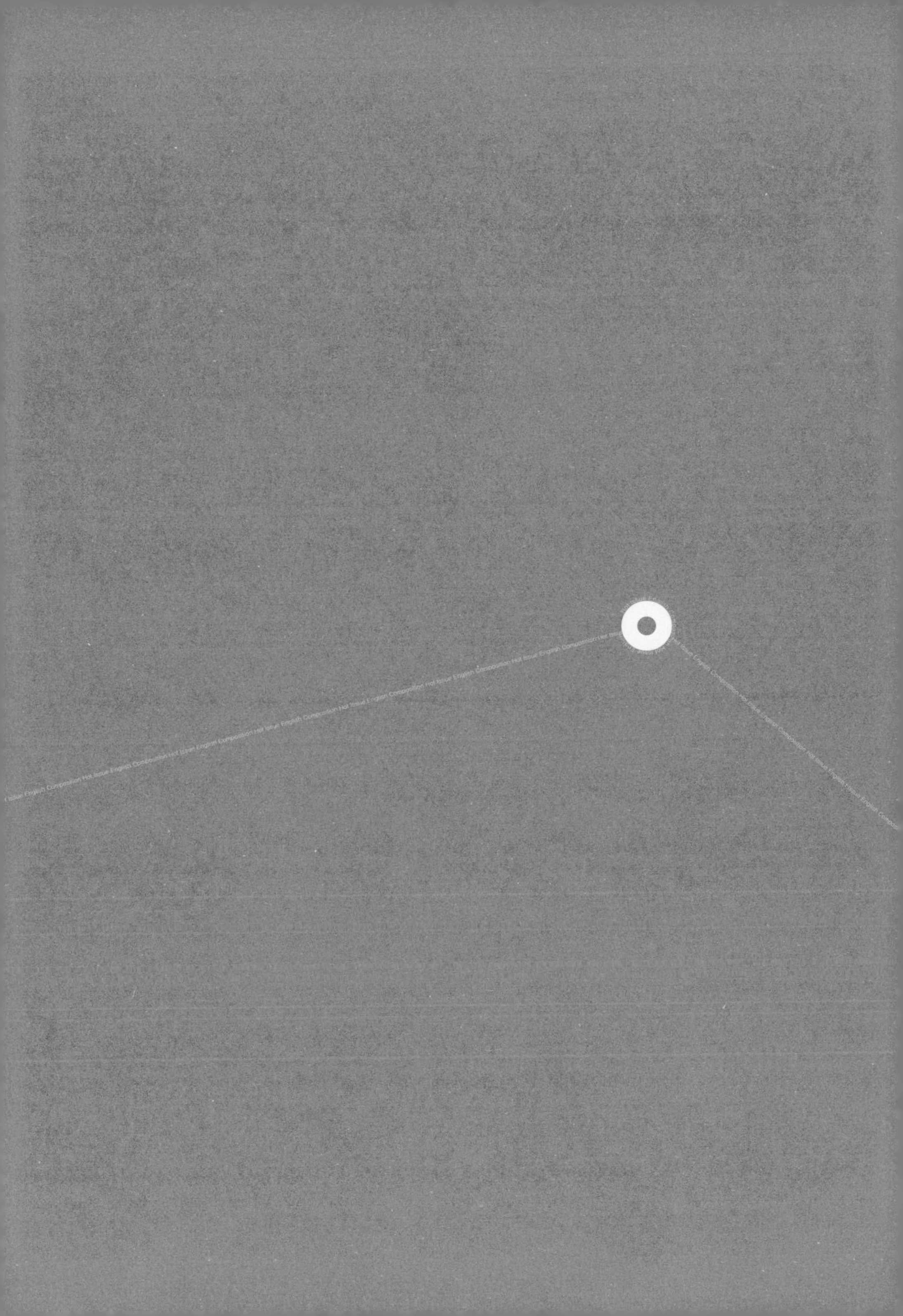

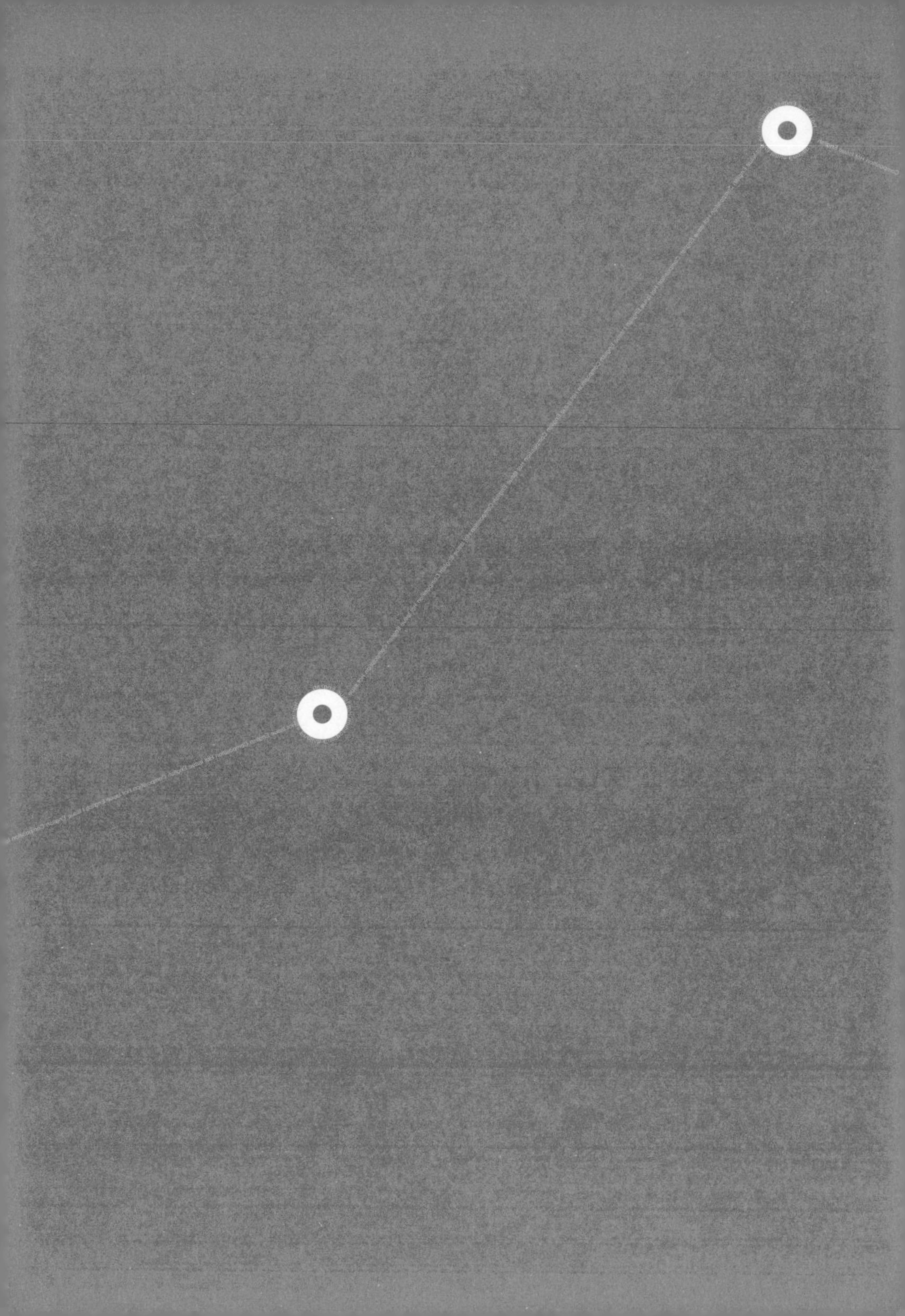

핫이슈 영작

Hot Issue English Composition
핫이슈 영작

1판 1쇄 발행 2016년 3월 10일

지은이 토마스 안·벨라 정
펴낸 곳 영어닷컴
디자인 공존
주소 서울시 종로구 삼봉로 95 대성 102-1004(견지동)
전화 (02) 739 5333
팩스 (02) 739 5777
전자우편 youngodotcom@gmail.com

ISBN 979-11-85345-08-6 13740

Hot Issue English Composition

핫이슈 영작

영어닷컴

왜 핫이슈 문장으로 영작을 배우는가

모든 말과 글의 가장 중요한 기능은 의미전달이다. 전달이라는 기능면에서 생각하면 말이든 글이든 의도하는 바를 제대로 전하는 것이 관건이다. 모국어로 대화하면서조차 의미를 잘못 이해하여 때때로 문제가 일어나는데, 문화와 정서가 다른 영어에 있어서 이런 경우를 접하면 어떻게 상대에게 의사를 전달하면 좋은지, 어떻게 착오 없이 올바로 이해시킬지 당황하게 된다.

하지만 가장 중요한 기능이 무엇인지 진단한 이상 해결 방법 역시 그 범위 내에서 찾아야 한다. 전달이라는 기능을 최대로 활용하고 있는 언론에서는 '핫이슈' 형태로 속보를 전한다. 장문의 복잡한 기사도 단 한 줄의 제목으로 오해 없이 많은 정보를 전달한다. 여기에 우리가 찾는 힌트가 있다.

영작도 마찬가지로 한글이 아닌 영어다운 의미 전달에 중점을 두어야 한다. 핫이슈 제목은 물론 한글로 표기된 어떤 문장도 영어로 표현이 안 될 대상은 없다. 이 책은 이런 관점에서 영어작문 연습에 도움을 제공한다. 국내 일간지의 핫이슈 문장은 짧고 간단하지만 깊은 의미와 다양한 내용, 풍부한 어휘를 사용하기 때문에 명확한 의미 전달을 연습하는 영작 교재로서 최고의 도구다.

영작에서 의미 전달 다음으로 중요한 일은 주어를 선정하는 일이다. 무엇을 주어로 정하느냐에 따라 전달력의 강약이 달라지고 의미의 선명도에 차이가 난다. 그 이외에 정확한 단어를 사용하여 원어민 입장에서 익숙한 표현을 하면 의미를 제대로 드러낼 수 있다. 특히 중요하다고 할 수 있는 전치사를 어법 사용에 맞추면서 물이 흐르듯이 자연스럽고 매끄럽게 문장을 이어가는 것이 영작의 요소들이라고 할 수 있다.

♀ 위에서 말한 영작의 핵심 기능과 주요 요소들을 염두에 두면서 《핫이슈 영작》과 더불어 편안하게 영작을 연습해보자. 본문에서는 국내 일간지의 최신기사로 전하는 핫이슈를 영작의 소재로 제시한다. 영어작문을 하는 방법은 한글 문장의 의미를 어떻게 영어로 표현할 것인지 곰곰이 생각하면서 우선 적합한 어휘를 찾는다. 다음 단계로 구문을 구성해본다. 마지막으로 영문을 만들기 위해 구문들을 이어 맞추어 완성한다.

♀ 한글이든 영문이든 작문이란 창의력을 동원하는 매우 흥미로운 작업이다. 이 책은 흥미를 유지하면서 편하게 작문을 할 수 있는 내용을 선호한다. 핫이슈 제목을 포함한 왼쪽 페이지는 영작 연습의 예(Writing Practice)를 제시하기 때문에 어색할 수도 있고 불완전할 수도 있고 서투를 수도 있지만, 단어 도출부터 의미 전달에 집중하며 한 문장을 끝까지 완성해보자.

♀ 'Writing Practice'는 영작을 위한 핵심 요소들의 완성도를 기준으로 평가한다. 따라서 완벽하지 않더라도 의미 전달에 문제가 적

으면 평균(80%) 정도의 평가를 받는다. 또한 부족한 부분을 수정함으로써 어떻게 문장이 좋아지는지 'Correction(%)'에서 확인이 가능하다.

♀ 한글 핫이슈를 영작연습(Writing practice), 수정(Correction) 및 예문(Model sentence)과 대조하여 차이를 느끼는 것만으로도 크게 발전할 수 있을 뿐만 아니라 이런 식의 연습으로 90% 이상의 성공도 기대할 수 있다.

♀ 이제 영작에서 가장 중요한 의미 전달을 위해 명확하게 의사를 표현하는 좋은 영작의 핵심 요령을 살펴보자.

영어작문을 위한 핵심 요령(본문 평가 기준100%)

1 의미가 명확하게 전달되는가 (Accurate meaning 50%)

2 주어 선정이 올바른가 (Subject selection 20%)

3 정확한 단어를 사용하는가 (Accurate word 5%)

4 익숙한 표현을 사용하는가 (Familiar expression 5%)

5 기본문장에 충실한가 (True to principal of sentence 5%)

6 쉬운 단어로 간단하게 표현하는가 (Simplified word 5%)

7 문장이 물과 같이 흐르는가 (Flowing and streaming 5%)

8 전치사 사용이 어법에 맞는가 (Usage of preposition 5%)

영작에서 문법을 먼저 생각하면 안 된다(의미 전달 방해)

1 영어문장의 5형식을 먼저 떠올려서는 안 된다

1형식, 2형식, 3형식, 4형식, 5형식

2 영어문장의 종류를 먼저 생각해서는 안 된다

단문, 중문, 복문

3 문법용어를 먼저 떠올리면 안 된다

등위접속사, 종속접속사, 형용사구, 부사절 등

4 전달하려는 내용 이외의 것을 먼저 생각하면 방해된다

어순, 도치, 문장분석, 공식 등

5 영어의 용도 구분은 거의 필요하지 않다

비즈니스용, 무역용, 전문 · 전공교육용, 회화용 등

❶ 핫이슈 문장

❷ Words 영작을 위한 주요 단어

❸ Phrases 영작을 위한 주요 구문

❹ Writing practice 영작 연습 문장

❺ Correction 영작 수정 문장

: Writing practice가 90% 이상이면 추가 수정은 하지 않는다

❻ Lecture 올바른 영작을 위한 핵심 사항을 살펴본다

❼ Model Sentence 최종적으로 제시하는 영작 예문

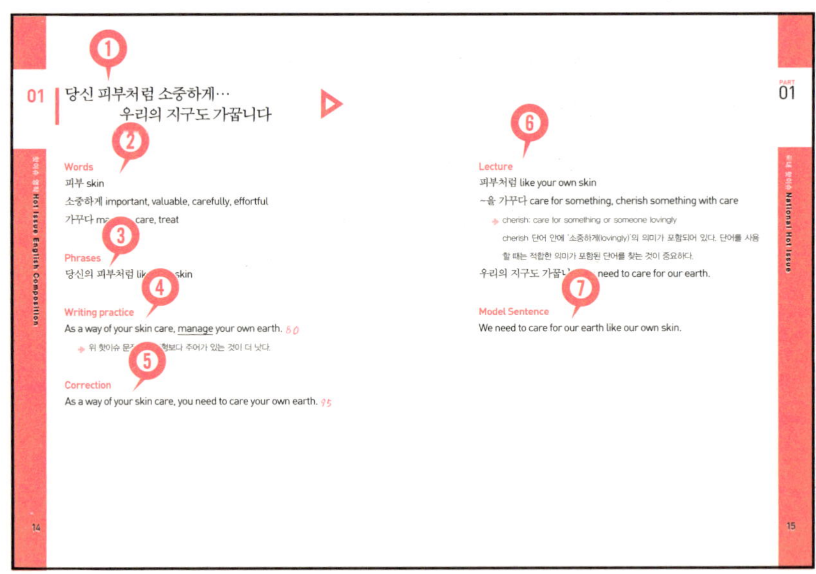

contents

part 01 국내 핫이슈

National Hot Issue

Words

피부 skin

소중하게 important, valuable, carefully, effortful

가꾸다 manage, care, treat

Phrases

당신의 피부처럼 like your skin

Writing practice

As a way of your skin care, <u>manage</u> your own earth. *80*

➜ 위 핫이슈 문장은 명령형보다 주어가 있는 것이 더 낫다.

Correction

As a way of your skin care, you need to care your own earth. *95*

Lecture

피부처럼 like your own skin

~을 가꾸다 care for something, cherish something with care

→ cherish: care for something or someone lovingly

cherish 단어 안에 '소중하게(lovingly)'의 의미가 포함되어 있다. 단어를 사용

할 때는 적합한 의미가 포함된 단어를 찾는 것이 중요하다.

우리의 지구도 가꿉니다 we need to care for our earth.

Model Sentence

We need to care for our earth like our own skin.

농식품 분야는
청년 일자리 블루오션

Words

농식품 agricultural industry

분야 sector

일자리 job opportunity

블루오션 blue ocean

Phrases

농식품 분야 agricultural industry sector

청년 일자리 young job opportunity

Writing practice

The sector of agricultural industry is blue ocean <u>for young job opportunity</u>. *85*

➜ 올바른 어법에 맞추어 쓴다.

Correction

The sector of agricultural industry is blue ocean of job opportunity for youth. *95*

Lecture

블루오션 blue ocean, blue ocean strategy (시장에서 성공할 수 있는 방법을 찾는 전략)
청년 일자리 job for the youth
농식품 분야 agricultural food field

➡ '농식품 분야는 청년 일자리 블루오션을 제공한다'는 의미에서 동사 provide를 사용한다.

Model Sentence

The field of agricultural food provides us with jobs for the youth.

03 | 이념 따라 바뀌지 않는 제대로 된 통일교육을

Words

이념 ideology

통일 unification

Phrases

이념에 따라 by ideology

바뀌지 않는 unchanged

제대로 된 unified, reasonable (합리적인, 분별이 있는, 타당한)

통일교육 education for unification

Writing practice

You need a <u>reasonable</u> education <u>for</u> unification that is unchanged by ideology. *85*

➔ 적합한 단어 사용이 필요하다

reasonable: 합리적인 right: 올바른

Correction

You need a right education of unification that does not change by ideology. *95*

20

Lecture

이념 ideology

이념 따라 by ideology

바뀌지 않는 unchanged

통일교육 unification education

준비하다, 마련하다 prepare, arrange

제대로 된 통일교육 upright education of unification, right education

➜ 'It is time that~'의 패턴을 이용한다.

이념 따라 바뀌지 않는 올바른 통일교육을 마련할 시기다.

Model Sentence

It is just time that we should arrange right education of unification.

비용만 절감 안전은 불감…
"저비용항공 정비 강화해야"

Words

절감 reduction, 안전 security

저비용 low fare, 항공 air flight

정비 maintenance, repair

강화 strengthen, tighten

Phrases

비용만 절감 reduce only cost

안전은 불감 unaware for security

저비용항공 정비 repair system for low flight fare

Writing practice

It needs to focus on <u>repairing system</u> on low fare flight, because they don't try to be aware of security, <u>but reduce</u> only cost. *80*

➡ 제도 수리가 아니라 정비 강화의 의미다.

Correction

It needs to focus on strengthening maintenance on low fare flight, because they don't try to be aware of security, but reducing only cost. *85*

Lecture

비용만 절감 cutting down on only cost, reduce only cost

안전은 불감 insensitive to safety, safety is unresponsive, unresponsive safety

➜ 비용은 절감 안전은 불감 cutting down on cost and insensitivity to safe followed

저비용항공 low cost flight

정비강화 strengthen its maintenance

비용만 절감하고 안전은 불감인 저비용 항공은 정비를 강화해야 한다.

Model Sentence

1. With only cost being reduced and its safety unresponsive, the low priced flight need reinforcing its maintenance.

2. The low cost airlines, cutting down on only price, and insensitive to the safety, are required to strengthen their maintenance.

05 | 소녀상은 '합의' 바깥에 앉아 있다

Words

소녀상 a statue of girl

합의 agreement, deal

Phrases

합의 바깥에 out of agreement

Writing practice

<u>The statue of girl</u> is sitting out of agreement between two countries. *90*

➜ 맞는 문장이지만 보다 간단한 표현이 더 좋다.

Correction

The girl statue is sitting out of agreement between two countries. *95*

Lecture

소녀상 girl statue

합의 agreement

바깥에 out of

➡ 그것은 합의 사항에 포함되어 있지 않다.

It is not included in the agreement. It is beyond the agreement.

Model Sentence

The girl statue is sitting out of the agreement

대기업 파견금지,
법으로 못박는다

Words

대기업 big company

파견 dispatch, send

금지 forbid, ban

파견금지 anti-dispatch

못 nail, peg, spike

Phrases

못 박다(고정시키다) nail, pin down to

쐐기를 박다, 강요하다 force, drive a wedge

Writing practice

<u>Anti-dispatch to big company</u> will be forced by law. *80*

➡ 한글 의미에 가까울수록 바람직하다.

Correction

Sending workers to big company will be banned by law. *90*

Lecture

대기업 major company

근로자 파견 금지 ban dispatched workers to major company

➡ Dispatched workers to major company is banned by law.

법으로 못 박다 It is nailed down into the law.

➡ 당국은 마감일을 내일로 못 박았다.

The authorities nailed down the deadline to tomorrow.

Model Sentence

It is nailed down into the law that dispatched workers to major companies are banned.

Words

사드(고고도 미사일 방어시스템) THAAD: Terminal High Altitude Area Defense Missile

한반도 Korean peninsular

배치 deployment, placement, position, station

Phrases

곤 (금방) as soon as possible, immediately, instantly, shortly

가시화 able to vision

Writing practice

The deployment of Thaad is <u>to see</u> in Korean peninsula as soon as possible. *80*

> ➡ '보여진다'와 '보다'는 차이가 크다.

Correction

The deployment of Thaad on Korean peninsula is to be seen as soon as possible. *90*

Lecture

사드 THAAD (Terminal High Altitude Area Defense)

한반도 배치 Deployment of Thaad on Korean peninsula

가시화되다 be on track

→ 로봇산업이 가시화되고 있다

Robot industries are on track.

Robot industries will soon come into vision.

Model Sentence

The deployment of Thaad on Korean peninsula will be soon on track.

08

"한국형 전투기 10년 내 개발 끝낸다"

Words

한국형 Korean type

전투기 a fighter, warplane

10년 내 within 10 years

개발 development

끝낸다 end, finish

Phrases

개발 끝낸다 end the development

Writing practice

It will end the development of a fighter Korean type within 10 years. *75*

→ 적합한 단어 선정이 필수 end: destroy, final

Correction

The development of a fighter Korean type will be finished within 10 years. *90*

Lecture

한국형 전투기 Jet fighter of Korean model plan(KF-X)
10년 내 끝낸다 will be completed in 10 years, will be wrapped up in 10 years

➡ 그 토론은 이미 끝났다 The debate has already been wrapped up.

➡ 성공적인 결론을 내다 wrap something up

개발이 끝나다 wrap up development

Model Sentence

Jet fighter of Korean model plan (KF-X), will be completed in 10 years.

09

방위사업청과 한국항공우주산업(KAI)이 우여곡절 끝에 한국형 전투기(KF-X) 사업의 시동을 걸었다

Words

방위사업청(DAPA) Defense Acquisition Program Administration

한국항공우주산업(KAI) Korea Aerospace Industries

우여곡절 turns and twists, complications

한국형 전투기(KF-X) 사업 Korean Fighter eXeperimental

시동 starting

Phrases

시동을 걸다 turn on the ignition

Writing practice

After <u>end of complications</u>, DAPA and KAI are to turn on the ignition on KF-X project. 80

➡ '우여곡절을 겪은 후에'의 한글의 의미를 보다 정확하게 옮길 필요가 있다.

Correction

After series of complications, DAPA and KAI are to turn on the ignition on KF-X project. 90

Lecture

방위사업청 Defense Business Service

한국항공우주산업 Korea Aerospace Industry

우여곡절 끝에 after many twists and turns

사업의 시동을 걸다 start undertaking

Model Sentence

Korean model jet fighter (KF-X) undertaking started just after many twists and turns between Defense Project Service and Korea Aerospace Industry.

10

드론 시범사업
빠르면 내달 말 뜬다

핫이슈 영작 Hot Issue English Composition

Words

드론 drone

시범 showing an example, model

사업 business, project

Phrases

빠르면 as early as

내달 말 late next month

뜨다(나오다, 시작되다) come out, appear

Writing practice

The model of drone project will appear <u>the end of</u> next month at earliest. *85*

> ➔ end 사용에 주의한다. '월말'에서 '~말'의 의미는 late가 적합하고, the end of 는 '마지막 날'이라는 의미다.

> ➔ 뜨다: 띄우다

Correction

The model of drone project will appear as early as late next month at earliest. *90*

Lecture

시범사업 model program

빠르면 if early

내달 말 late next month

뜨다 float in the sky

시범사업이 빠르면 if model project is programmed early

드론이 뜨다 drone will fly

- ➡ drone은 동사로도 사용된다. 즉 move with a continuous humming sound (계속 윙윙하는 소리를 내면서 움직이다)
- ➡ Traffic droned up and down the street. 차 소리가 계속 길 위아래로 윙윙 소리를 내면서 지나갔다.

Model Sentence

If drone model project is programmed early, the drone will fly late next month.

11

'보이스피싱과 즐거운 대화'라는 제목의 영상은 유튜브에서 45만 건의 조회 수 기록하며 화제가 됐다

Words

보이스피싱 voice phishing

즐거운 pleasant, happy, merry

대화 conversation, talking

영상(동영상) video, clip

유튜브(전 세계 최대 무료 동영상 공유 사이트) YouTuve

조회 수(클릭 수) click

화제 topic, issue

Phrases

조회 수를 기록하다 record the number of click

Writing practice

The video titled "The joyful talk with voice phishing" recored 450,000 clicks on YouTube, making topic. *95*

Lecture

보이스피싱 voice phishing

즐거운 대화 joyful talk

제목의 영상 image titled

유튜브에서 45만 건의 조회수 four hundred fifty thousands of people visited the site on YouTube

Model Sentence

The image titled "joyful conversation with a voice phishing" has got 450,000 hits on YouTube, and is now the talk of the town.

12

또 뚫린 인천공항,
소 잃고 외양간도 못 고치나

Words

뚫리다 unchecked, be passed

인천공항 Inchon International Airport

Phrases

소 잃고 외양간 고치다(~격이다) with the wisdom of hindsight, "close the barn door after the horse has bolted"

Writing practice

Inchon International Airport has passed unchecked <u>something</u> again, why doesn't change the way that "mend the barn door after the horse has bolted" *80*

> ➡ something을 가리키는 it가 빠져있다: doesn't it change

Correction

Inchon International Airport has passed unchecked again, why doesn't it change the way that "close the barn door after the horse has bolted." *90*

Lecture

뚫다 break through

소 잃고 외양간 고치다 shut the stable door after the horse has bolted

→ '외양간도 못 고치나'는 '소를 잃어버렸으면 외양간은 고쳐야 되지 않나'의 의미

소 잃고 외양간도 못 고치나 the faulty stable should have been mended at least if the horse had been bolted.

인천 공항이 또 뚫렸다 Inchon airport is slipping again.

→ slipping 정상적인 역할을 제대로 못 하는

Model Sentence

Inchon airport is again slipping. It should know better that it is too late to shut the stable door after the horse has bolted.

13

19년 전으로 갈 수 있다면…

Phrases

19년 전으로 19 years ago

갈 수 있다면 if it could come back

Writing practice

If I wish come back 19 years ago... *75*

> 19년 전으로 돌아갈 수 있다면: 가정법 과거 I could go back

Correction

I wish I could go back 19 years before... *90*

Lecture

가정법 'only if'패턴을 사용한다.

할 수만 있으면, 즉 지금으로서는 현실 불가능한 일을 의미한다.

- ➡ only if 현실 불가능한 경우, 실제로 과거에 듣지 않았다.

- ➡ 너의 이야기만 들었더라면 If only I had listened to you.

- ➡ 'We wish we could' 표현도 사용할 수 있다.

- ➡ We wish we could listened to you.

Model Sentence

Only if we could go back 19 years before.

14

정치·경제·사회 생태계
늙고 황폐해져
극단적 고비용·저생산성 심화

Words

정치 politics, 경제 economic, 사회 society

Phrases

생태계가 늙어가다 ecosystem is getting older

황폐해지다 devastated

극단적 고비용 extreme high cost

저생산성 심화(되고 있다) deepening low producing

Writing practice

With politics, economic and society ecosystem <u>are</u> getting older and devastate, extreme high price and low productivity is deepening. *85*

➡ 한 문장에 동사는 한 개만 존재하기 때문에 with절에서 are는 생략한다.

Correction

With politics, economic and society ecosystem getting older and devastated, extreme high price and low productivity are deepening. *95*

Lecture

정치·경제·사회 politics and economic society ecology
생태계가 늙어가다 ecosystem is becoming old
황폐해지다 devastated
고비용·저생산성 high cost and low productivity
심화되고 있다 deepening
정치·경제·사회 생태계가 늙고 황폐해지고 있으므로 고비용·저생산성이 심화되고 있다.

Model Sentence

As the politics and economic society ecosystem is getting older and devastated, high cost and low productivity are deepening.

15

한국, 차별화 경쟁력
중·일보다 높지만 역전 위험

Words

차별 discrimination

경쟁력 competition power

역전 reversal, turnabout

Writing practice

Korea remains risk, though it has <u>on highly</u> discrimination and competition than China and Japan. *80*

➡ 한글 문장의 의미를 명확히 파악한다; 차별화된 경쟁력

Correction

Korea remains risk, though it has higher discrimination competitive power than China and Japan. *95*

Lecture

차별화 경쟁력 discrimination competitive edge

중·일보다 높다 higher discrimination competitive edge than in Japan and China

역전위험 situation may reverse, situation may threat to disfavor Korea.

➡ The system favors those who employ less labor and disfavors those who employ more. 그 제도는 직원을 적게 고용하는 회사에는 유리하고 많은 직원을 고용하는 회사에는 불리하다.

Model Sentence

Korea has the higher competitive edge of discrimination than Japan or China has, but situation may threat to reverse.

지금이 국가 구조조정의 천금의 기회, 추락한 국가 리더십 다시 세워야

Words

리더십 leadership

세우다 set up

추락하다 drop, fall, crash

Phrases

구조조정 structural regulation, restructuring

천금의 기회(황금의 기회) golden opportunity

Writing practice

It is golden time for national restructure to set up our fallen state's leadership again. *95*

Lecture

국가 구조조정 national organization structuring

천금의 기회 golden opportunity

추락한 국가 리더십 fallen national leadership

다시 세우다 put to rights

→ The government attempted to put the economy to rights. 그 정부는 경제
를 바로 잡으려고 노력했다.

Model Sentence

It is time of the golden opportunity for national organization
structuring, and we must put national falling leadership to rights.

 한 · 미 · 일 6자회담 셔틀외교 시작된 날, 북한 무인기 띄웠다 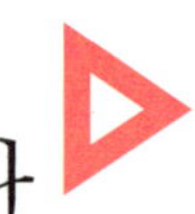

Words

무인기(드론) drone

띄우다 fly, float

Phrases

6자 회담 the 6 party talks

셔틀외교 shuttle diplomacy

Writing practice

<u>When the day</u> had started the shuttle diplomacy of the six party talks, drones were floated by North Korea. *85*

➤ when the day는 잘못된 표현이다.

Correction

On the day Korea, the U.S. and Japan started their shuttle diplomacy for the six party talks, North Korea flied drone. *95*

Lecture

6자 회담 the 6 party talks

셔틀외교 shuttle diplomacy

시작하다 resume

무인기 띄우다 fly drone

> ➜ fly는 '비행기로 여행을 하다'의 의미도 있다.
>
> I fly back to Seoul this evening. 오늘 저녁 비행기로 서울에 돌아간다.
>
> ➜ flow는 '비행기로 수송하다'는 의미다.
>
> Helicopters flew the injured to hospital. 헬리콥터들이 부상자들을 병원으로 수송했다.

무인기를 띄우다 fly drone

Model Sentence

On the day when Korea, the U.S. and Japan resumed their shuttle diplomacy of 6 part talks, North Korea flied drone up.

이란 수출길 넓어진 한국 차 수요 확대 힘찬 시동 걸었다

Words

수출길 the way of export

넓어지다 get board

수요 demand

확대 increase, expand

Phrases

힘찬(활기 찬) active, energetic, dynamic

시동을 걸다 make a machine start, turn on switch

Writing practice

Korean cars being widen export way to Iran has started the increasing demand vigorously. *80*

> being widen을 being widened로, 'and' 또는 ';'으로 나누면 뜻이 분명해진다.

Correction

Korean cars export being widened; the way to Iran has started the increasing demand vigorously. *85*

Lecture

이란 수출길이 넓어지다 the route of export to Iran

한국 차 수효 확대 the demand of Korean cars expands

힘찬 시동을 걸다 take a powerful starting

➡ route는 도로와 철도에서 사용

Proposals have been put forward for a new route around the south of the town.

이 마을 주위에 새로운 길(도로)을 만드는 안건이 제출되었다.

Model Sentence

The route for the export to Iran has been widened for Korean cars, and the expansion of their demand takes a powerful starting.

19 | 저성장시대 시장흐름 맞게
사업구조 빨리 고도화해야

Words

저성장시대 low growth era

시장흐름 market flowing

사업구조 corporal structure

고도화하다(높은 수준으로 향상하다) advance, upgrade

Phrases

흐름에 맞춰 adjusting to flowing

Writing practice

The corporal structure needs to upgrade <u>adjust on</u> market flowing at the low growth era. *85*

→ adjust on보다는 adjust to가 더 적절하다

Correction

The business structure needs to upgrade adjusting to market flowing at the low growth era. *90*

Lecture

저성장시대 the period of the low growth rate

시장흐름을 맞추다 adjust to the flow of markets

사업구조 business structure

사업구조를 고도화하다 achieve a high level of the business structure

Model Sentence

Business structure would have to achieve its high level adjusting to the market of the period of the low growth rate.

20

계약직 근로자는 속 타고,
기업은 뒤에서 표정 관리

Words

계약 contract

근로자 worker, labor

속 타다 worry, be distressed

기업 company

뒤에서 behind

Phrases

표정 관리 control of facial expression

계약직 근로자 part time worker, irregular job

Writing practice

Many <u>part-time workers</u> are distressed in their inside, on the other hand the companies is controlling its expression behind. *85*

➡ part-time work: 시간제 아르바이트, contract labor: 계약직 근로자

Correction

The contract labors are distressed in their inside and, on the other hand, companies is controlling its expression behind. *90*

Lecture

계약직 근로자(인턴) contract labor

속 타다 to be distressed, be troubled

뒤에서 표정 관리하다 maintain self-discipline in their sleeve

> → Try not to show it on their faces.

> → 불쾌한 결과를 맞이하다(현 상황에 불평하다) face the music

Model Sentence

The contract labors are facing the music, and the companies are trying not to show on their faces.

21

복잡하고 석연찮은 대학입시

Words

복잡하다 complicate

석연찮은 not sure, unclear, be suspected

대학 college

입시 entrance examination

Writing practice

It is unclear and complicated exam system. *70*

> ➜ 석연하다: 마음에 걸리는 일이 풀려서 개운하다, 석연찮다: 의심스럽다

Correction

The college exam system is doubtful and complicated. *90*

Lecture

복잡한 complicated

석연찮은 doubtful

대학입시 college entrance exam

➜ 대학입시는 복잡하고 석연치 않다

석연치 않다 (이해가 안 된다) do not quite make sense

Model Sentence

The college entrance examination is complicated and does not quite make sense.

22 ICT레저 옷 입은 농업, 21세기 풍년가 부른다

Words

ICT(정보통신 기술) Information Communication Technology

레저 leisure, 농업 agriculture

21세기 21 century

풍년가 the song of bumper year

Phrases

노래를 부르다 sing a song

풍년가를 부르다 sing a song of bumper

옷을 입다 wear clothes

Writing practice

The part of agriculture wearing ICT leisure <u>is singing</u> a song of bumper year of the 21 century. *85*

➡ 한글 의미를 명확하게 파악해야 한다: ICT레저 옷을 입은 농업

Correction

The part of agriculture wearing ICT leisure clothes is singing a song of bumper year of the 21 century. *90*

Lecture

ICT leisure clothes

풍년가 bumper year song

레저산업 leisure industry

- ➜ 이 레저 옷들은 싸게 판다 This leisure clothes sell at low prices.
- ➜ 레저 활동 leisure activity
- ➜ 우울하거나 힘이 없는 low depressed or lacking in energy
- ➜ 그는 힘이 없어 보였다 He was feeling low.

Model Sentence

Farming wearing ICT leisure clothes sing the bumper year song.

한 발 늦었지만,
한국이 잘하는 의료·가전·교육
AI(Artificial Intelligence)에 집중하라

Words

한 발 one step, 늦다 late, 잘하다 well done, good

의료 medicine, 가전 electric home appliances, 교육 education

AI(인공지능에 제공받는 서비스) Artificial Intelligence

집중하라 focus

Writing practice

Although we are <u>late one step</u> now, Korea is <u>able to focus</u> on
our skillful part such as medicine, electric home appliances and
education. *85*

➡ 어법에 맞는 위치: one step late, 간단한 표현이 좋다: to focus

➡ '한발 늦었지만'의 의미는 뒤쳐졌다는 뜻이다.

➡ 되도록 간단한 표현이 좋다.

Correction

Although we are one step behind, Korea has to focus on our
skillful part such as medicine, electric home appliances and
education. *90*

Lecture

한발 늦었지만 although it is a little late

집중하다 focus on

한국이 잘하는 medicine, home appliances and education which Korea is good at

Model Sentence

Korea may well have to focus on medicine, home appliances and education that he is good at, although it is a little late.

모든 지하철역 주변
4월부터 금연

Words

지하철역 주변 around subway station

금연 non smoking

Phrases

모든 지하철역 주변 all of around subway stations

Writing practice

Non-smoking is implemented for all of <u>surrounding</u> of subway stations from this April. *80*

➡ 한글 의미에 보다 가깝게 표현하는 것이 필요하다. 금연: 흡연이 금지된다.

➡ 주변: around, 둘러싸다: surround

Correction

Smoking is banned around all subway stations from this April. *95*

Lecture

지하철 주변 around subways

4월부터 금연 smoking is not allowed starting April

➜ allow의 의미는 '어떤 장소에 들어가는 것을 허용하다'이다.

let someone enter a place or go in a particular direction.

➜ The river was patrolled and few people were allowed across.

그 강에는 순찰 도는 사람이 있었고, 아무도 그 강을 건너는 것이 허용되지 않았다.

Model Sentence

Smoking is not allowed around all subway surrounding starting April.

25

어머니 말기 암 가슴 사무쳐…
암 신약 개발에 10억 냈죠

Words

말기 암 the end of cancer stage, terminal stage of cancer

암 신약 new cancer medicine

개발 develop

10억 1 billion

내다 give, contribute

Phrases

가슴에 사무치다 painful in his heart

Writing practice

<u>Since</u> mother's terminal cancer had made me painful in my heart,

I <u>paid off</u> one billion won for developing new cancer medicine. *85*

> ➜ pay off: (빚 진 것을) 갚다, 위의 핫이슈 의미는 '기부하다'는 의미다.

Correction

Because mother's terminal cancer had made me painful in my

heart, I gave one billion won for developing new cancer medicine.

95

Lecture

말기 암 terminal cancer

암 신약 개발 development of new cancer medicine

10억을 내다 contribute one billion won

어머니의 말기 암이 가슴에 사무쳐 my mother's terminal cancer sinking deep in my mind

Model Sentence

My mother's terminal cancer sinking deep in my mind, I rushed to contribute a billion won to developing new medicine for cancer.

26

행동 느리고 손재주 없는 콤플렉스가 나를 만들었다

Words

행동 act, behavior, moving

손재주 hand skill

콤플렉스 a complex, weakness, shortcoming, disadvantage

Phrases

나를 만들다 (성공하게 만들다) make me success

Writing practice

My weakness such as <u>slow moving</u> and <u>lack of hand skill</u> served to achieve the success now. *80*

> ➜ move: 옮기다, 이사하다, 이동하다
>
> ➜ slow moving는 물체가 서서히 움직인다는 의미이고, slow action은 동작이 느리다는 의미다.

Correction

My weakness of being slow action and all thumbs, served to achieve my success now. *85*

Lecture

행동이 느리다 slow in action

콤플렉스 complex

손재주가 없다 all thumbs

Model Sentence

Having a complex about being slow in action and all thumbs made me what I am today.

27

2025년 신고속철 시대, 서울 – 속초 90분 주파

Words

고속철(고속철도) rapid transit railway

자기부상 철도 magnetic levitation train

주파하다 run the whole distance, run

Writing practice

2025 year is era new magnetic levitation train running between Seoul and Sokcho <u>for</u> 90 minutes. *85*

➜ for 90 minutes: 90분 동안, in 90 minutes: 90분 이내에

Correction

2025 year is era of new magnetic levitation train running between Seoul and Sokcho in 90 minutes. *90*

Lecture

신고속철 New High-Speed train

시대 era

신고속철 an era of New High-Speed train

2025년은 신고속철 시대로 접어든다 2025 year ushers in an era of new high-speed train.

→ usher something in 어떤 새로운 것의 시작이 되다

→ The railways ushered in an area of cheap mass travel.

서울–속초를 90분에 주파한다 It runs Seoul to Sokcho in 90 minutes.

Model Sentence

2025 year ushers in an era of new high-speed train, which runs Seoul to Sokcho in 90 minutes.

part 02 국제 핫이슈

International Hot Issue

사우디, 이란과 단교…
"누가 먼저 죽나" 2차 석유전쟁

Words

단교 break up relationship, separate

Phrases

누가 먼저 죽나 Who will die first

2차 석유전쟁 the second oil war

Writing practice

With breaking up their relationship between Saudi Arabia and Iran, it has started the second oil war <u>whoever</u> will die first. *85*

> ➜ 영어문장은 물처럼 매끄럽게 흐르고 간단하게 쓰는 것이 좋다.

> ➜ 개인관계는 relationship이고, 국가간의 관계는 relations를 주로 사용한다.

Correction

With breaking up their relations between Saudi Arabia and Iran, it has started the second oil war ending who will die first. *90*

72

국제 핫이슈 International Hot Issue

Lecture

국교 단절 sever a diplomatic relations

누가 먼저 죽나? Who will die first?

2차 석유 전쟁 the second oil war

2차 석유전쟁에 접어들다 enter the 2nd oil war

→ 사우디와 이란은 국교단절을 하고 누가 먼저 죽나 경쟁을 하며 2차 석유전쟁에 접어들었다.

Model Sentence

Saudi severs its diplomatic relations with Iran. Both compete who dies first. They have just entered 2nd oil war.

02 "와인 없이 어떻게"
"술은 내놓지 마라"
올랑드·로하니, 오찬 대신 맹물 만남

Words

오찬 luncheon, 올랑드(프랑스 대통령) Francois Hollande
로하니(이란 대통령) Hassan Rouhani

Phrases

와인 없이 어떻게 즐길까 how we have enjoy without wine
술은 내놓지 마라 don't offer wine
오찬 대신 instead of luncheon, 맹물 만남 meeting with only water

Writing practice

It has become a meeting with only water instead of luncheon
after arranging on different ideas between wondering talking with
no wine by Hollande and saying no thanks on any kind of one by
Hassan Rouhani. 80

➜ 복잡한 장문보다 간결한 문장으로 표현하는 것이 더 이해하기 쉽다.

Correction

It has become a meeting with only water instead of luncheon,
because Hollande insisted wondering on talking with no wine,
and Hassan Rouhani said no thanks on any kind of it. 90

Lecture

와인 없이 어떻게 how is it without wine
술은 내놓지 마라 don't offer drink
오찬 대신 맹물 만남 meet nonalcoholic drink, not luncheon

Model Sentence

How is it without wine? Francois Hollande argued; "don't let drink out" Hassan Rouhani said; and then both ended up with meeting non-alcoholic drink, not a luncheon.

중국 "소로스는 자본주의 악당" 헤지펀드와 전쟁 선포

Words

소로스(금융 투자 전문가) George Soros
자본주의 capitalism, 악당 rogue, villain
헤지펀드(파생금융상품) hedge fund, (최소의 손실로 최대의 이익을 얻음)
선포 declare, announcement

Phrases

헤지펀드와 전쟁 선포 declare a war against hedge fund
자본주의 악당 rogue of capitalism

Writing practice

China declares a war against hedge fund, viewing Soros as a rogue of capitalism. *95*

Lecture

비난하다 criticize, Soros

자본주의 악당 capitalistic bad guy

전쟁 선포 declare war against hedge-fund

비난하다 criticize, 또는 blame, condemn

비난을 피하다 dodge criticism

➡ 그 나라는 국제법을 어겼다는 비난을 피할 수가 없다. The country can't possibly avoid being criticized for violating international laws.

Model Sentence

China declared a war against hedge-fund condemning Soros as capitalistic bad guy.

 오바마
"감히 우리 동맹 공격하면 파멸"

Words

오바마 (미국 대통령) Barack Obama

감히 dare, boldly

동맹 alliance, ally

공격 attack, aggression, strike

파멸 ruin, destruct, wreck

Phrases

동맹 공격하면 when someone attack one of our allies

Writing practice

Obama said that whoever attacks one of our allies <u>boldly</u> will end ruin. *80*

➡ 감히: dare 대담하게, 과감히: boldly

Correction

Obama said whoever dares to attack one of our allies, will end up ruining. *95*

Lecture

우리 동맹 our ally

동맹을 맺다 form alliance

동맹을 공격하다 attack ally

파멸을 가져올 것이다 will be destabilized or strayed, will be ruined

➡ 오바마는 만약 누군가가 우리 동맹을 공격하면 파멸시키겠다고 말했다.

Model Sentence

Obama said that if someone attacks one of our allied, he shall be destroyed.

중국이 제재 미적대는 사이 미사일 꺼내든 북

Words

제재 sanctions
미적대다 mildness, lukewarm, tepid, half-hearted
미사일 missile

Phrases

제재를 미적대는 사이에 while it keeps in its lukewarm stance
미사일을 꺼내들다 hold up missile threating

Writing practice

While China keeps their stance in lukewarm, North Korea has held up its missile threating. *80*

> ➜ 동명사 threating보다는 명사 threat가 더 적절하다.

Correction

While China keeps their stance in lukewarm, North Korea has pulled out its missile threat. *95*

Lecture

제재를 미적대다 goof off sanctions

미사일을 꺼내 들다 pull missile

미적거리다 drag one's feet

그들은 서로 눈치를 보며 미적거렸다 They shifted around and stole glances at each other.

➡ 미적거리다 shift around 눈치를 보다 steal glances

Model Sentence

North Korea pulled out missiles when China keeps goofing off sanctions.

06

최강 막말 콤비 탄생

Words

최강 the most powerful

막말 a blunt remark, rude talk, careless talk

콤비 combination, a pare, a duo

탄생 be born, come out, rise

Phrases

최강 콤비 the most powerful pare

Writing practice

Coming out the most powerful <u>rude talking</u> duo in public. *80*

➡ rude talking duo는 '막말을 하고 있는 두 사람'의 의미로 한글 의미와 차이가 있다.

Correction

The most powerful rude talk duo was born. *85*

Lecture

최강 the strongest, the most powerful

막말(거친, 상스런, 난폭한) rough words, coarse

막말 또는 슬랭 rough words or slang English words

콤비 duo, double act

탄생 birth

탄생하다 come into the world

➜ 그들 사이에 막말이 오고갔다. Rough words were exchanged between them.

가장 강력하게 막말하는 콤비가 탄생했다.

Model Sentence

The strongest rough words double act has been born.

07

국내서 일한 외국인 7명, IS합류

Words

외국인 foreigner, expatriate
IS(급진 수니파 무장단체) Islamic State
합류하다 join

Phrases

국내서 일하다 work in domestic
IS에 합류하다 join in IS

Writing practice

Seven expatriates who had worked once in Korea joined <u>in</u> IS. *92*

> ➡ join은 in이 필요 없다.

Correction

Seven expatriates who had worked once in Korea joined IS. *95*

Lecture

국내에서 일한 외국인 foreigners who worked in Korea

합류하다 join

→ 무소속 의원들의 합류로 당의 지지도가 더 올라갔다.

With joining of the non-partisan assemblymen, the party has gained its credibility.

Model Sentence

Seven foreigners who worked in Korea have joined IS.

08

바다 떠다니는 기름 창고…
유조선이 동났다

Words

떠다니는 float

기름 창고 oil tanker

유조선 mega tanker

동났다 sold out, be exhausted

Phrases

바다를 떠다니다 ocean floating

유조선이 동났다 mega oil tankers sold out

Writing practice

Many of mega oil tankers which are floating on the sea, were sold

out. 90

Lecture

바다를 떠다니는 기름 창고 oil storage

유조선 oil tanker

동나다(없어지다, 바닥나다) give out, give something out, sold out

Model Sentence

Oil storage floating on the sea, the oil tankers sold out.

09

"우리가 무함마드 적통"
수니-시아파 1,400년 전쟁

Words

무함마드(마호메트: 이슬람 선지자) Muhammad

적통 descent legally

수니파(쿠란과 무함마드의 사위 알리를 추종하는 종파) Sunni
Muslim

시아파(무함마드의 혈통만 지도자 칼리파로 인정하는 종파) Shiite
Muslim

Phrases

무함마드 적통 Muhammad's descent legally

Writing practice

<u>Two parts</u> of Muslim-Sunni and Shiite are lasting for 1,400 year
<u>war</u>, insisting legal descent each other. *80*

➤ 주어 선정을 분명하게 해야 한다. two parts에는 between이 필요하다.

Correction

The war between two factions of Muslim-Sunni and Shiite are
lasting for 1,400 years, each insisting his legal descendant from
Muhammad. *90*

Lecture

무하마드 적통 Muhammad, direct descendant of Muhammad
1,400년의 수니파와 시아파 간의 다툼 1,400 years of fight between Sunni and Shia
종교전쟁 religious war

Model Sentence

Sunni and Shia has been fighting over claim insisting "We are direct descendant of Muhammad" for 1,400 years.

10

일본 무기 수입,
11년간 198조 원 쏟아 세계 1위

Words

무기 weapon, arms, arsenal

수입 import, procurement (조달, 획득)

쏟다 spend, appropriation (전용)

Phrases

무기 수입 arsenal import

세계 1위 top of the world

Writing practice

Japan's weaponry procurement is <u>top</u> of the world, with spending 198 trillion won for 11 years. *93*

→ top 대신 on the top이 더 좋은 표현이다.

Correction

Japan's weaponry procurement is on the top of the world, with spending 198 trillion won for 11 years. *95*

Lecture

무기수입 import weapon

세계 1위 rank world No.1

198조 원을 쏟아 붓다 pour 198 trillion won into

➡ '돈을 ~에 쏟아 붓다'의 의미로 spend money on 패턴을 이용하기도 한다.

11년간 over past 11 years

➡ pour something like money into 엄청난 돈을 ~에 투자하다

➡ contribute something like money to an enterprise or project in copious amount

많은, 풍부한 copious

Model Sentence

1. The import of weapon by Japan ranks number one in the world by pouring 198 trillion won.

2. Japan ranks world No. 1 in importing weapon by pouring 198 trillion won Into it

11 런던 월세 500만 원…
영국 의원, 집 대신 '보트살이'

Words

월세 monthly rent

영국 의원 a member of parliament (MP)

Phrases

월세 500만 원 monthly rent for 500 million won

보트살이 living on boat

Writing practice

London has priced monthly rent for 5 million won, so the Member
of Parliament is living on boat instead of house. *90*

Lecture

월세 monthly rent

영국의원 member of Parliament

보트살이 boat living

대신 instead of

→ walk to work instead of going by car 자동차 대신 걸어서 직장에 가다

런던 월세가 500만 원이어서 한 영국 의원은 집 대신에 보트에서 살고 있다.

Model Sentence

Monthly rent in London is 5 million won. One of British member of Parliaments is living on the boat instead of housing.

12 | 실리콘밸리 혁신 에너지 흐르는
미국 대표 명문 프린스턴

Words

실리콘밸리 Silicon Valley

혁신 innovate

명문 prestigious (명성 있는, 일류의)

프린스턴대학 Princeton

Phrases

에너지가 흐르는 energy running, flowing out energy, well up energy (에너지가 넘치는)

Writing practice

Princeton is one of prestigious schools in the U.S., where has been run <u>innovative energy in Silicon Valley</u>. *75*

➡ '혁신 에너지가 흐르는 실리콘 밸리'가 주어임을 감안하자.

Correction

Princeton is one of prestigious schools in the U.S. where the innovative energy of the Silicon Valley has been running over. *95*

Lecture

실리콘밸리 Silicon Valley

혁신 에너지가 흐르는 (혁신 에너지로 유명한) noted for Silicon Valley energy

미국의 명문 프린스턴 U.S. best prestigious University

Model Sentence

Silicon Valley innovative energy is felt throughout U.S. best prestigious Princeton University.

13

이란 찾은 시진핑 "교역 720조로 확대"하고 아베도 상반기 방문

Words

교역 trade, commerce, exchange

확대 rise, increase, expend

상반기 first half year

방문, 방문하다 visit

Phrases

교역 확대 increase trade

Writing practice

When Chinese President, Xi went to Iran, he expanded their trade into 720 trillion won, and then Japanese Prime Minister Abe makes a plan to visit in first half this year. 85

➔ make a plan 대신 plan을 동사로 사용하면 간단하다.

Correction

When Chinese President, Xi went to Iran, he expanded their trade into 720 trillion won, and then Japanese Prime Minister Abe plans to visit in first half this year. 95

Lecture

시진핑 Xi Jinping

아베 (일본 총리) Shinzo Abe

이란을 찾다 visit Iran

교역량을 720조로 확대하다 expand bilateral trade volume to 720 trillion won

아베도 상반기 방문 Japan prime minister Abe visit Iran in the first of this year.

Model Sentence

China president Xi Jinping visited Iran, expanding bilateral trade volume with Iran to 720 trillion won, and Japanese Prime Minister Abe will be visiting Iran in the first half of this year.

14

인구 1억 명 사수하는 일본 마지노선은 출산율 1.8%

핫이슈 영작 Hot Issue English Composition

Words

인구 population

사수하다(유지하다) keep, defend

마지노선(최후의 방어선, 마지노 요새: 독일을 방어하기 위해 앙드레 마지노 국방장관이 요청하여 만든 요새) Ligne Maginot(불어), the front line

출산율 birth rate

Writing practice

The front line of birth rate in Japan is 1.8 percentages point for sustaining 100 million populations. 75

➡ 주어를 잘 선택하면 좋은 영문이 된다.

Correction

The front line of birth rate in Japan is 1.8 percentages to sustain population of 100 million. 85

Lecture

인구 1억 명 population of one hundred million

사수하다 defend

인구 1억 명을 사수하는 일본 Japan, which defend its population of one hundred million

마지노선을 출산율 1.8%로 보다 see birth rate as the Maginot line

Model Sentence

Japan, which is defending its population of one hundred million, sees birth rate 1.8% as the Maginot line.

15 | 전 세계 7세 아이들 65%는 지금 없는 직업 가질 것

Words

전 세계 all of the world

직업 jobs

Phrases

지금 없는 직업 out of existing jobs

Writing practice

<u>Among 7 years old of the world now</u>, the percentage of 65 will be given out of existing jobs. *75*

➜ 좋은 영어문장은 주어가 좌우한다.

Correction

The 65 percentage of 7 years old children in the world now, will hold occupations which are non-existent at this moment. *85*

Lecture

전 세계 all of the world, entire world

7세 아이들 65%: 65% of 7 year-old children in the whole world

지금 없는 직업 occupation which doesn't exist right now

지금 없는 직업을 가지다 hold career we can't see at this moment

Model Sentence

The 65% of 7 year-old children in the whole world would have jobs that we don't have at this moment.

16

경기 풀리자 취업 훈풍
일본 대학 문과의 부활

Words

경기 economy

풀리다(나아지다) get better

취업 get a job

훈풍 go well

문과 the liberal arts

부활 revival

Writing practice

<u>Since</u> good economy draws better opportunity jobs, the liberal arts department in Japan is getting recovered. *75*

➜ since가 '～이래로'라는 의미로 사용되는 것을 피하기 위해 as를 사용한다.

Correction

As good economy is coming better opportunity jobs, the liberal arts department in Japanese colleges is getting recovered. *85*

Lecture

경기 풀리자 as economy is improving(picking up)

취업 훈풍(취업의 기회가 더 많아진) with more opportunity for employment

문과 the liberal arts

부활하다 revive

➜ 경기가 좋아지자 취업의 더 좋은 기회를 맞이한 일본 대학이 문과를 부활시키고 있다.

Model Sentence

1. As economy (business) is picking up, Japanese colleges are seeing the better opportunity for employment, and are reviving their liberal arts.

2. As business is improving, Japanese colleges with warm wind for employment are reviving their liberal arts.

17

중국 경제는 불안해도
기업의 기세는 무섭다

Words

경제 economy

불안 unstable

기업 industry, company, corporate

기세 power, force, influence

무섭다 scary, terrify, dread

Phrases

경제가 불안하다 economy is unstable

기업의 기세 influence of industry

Writing practice

Although Chinese economy is unstable, their industrial influence threats the rest of countries. *75*

> ➜ 정확한 단어를 사용할 것. threat: 위협하다

Correction

Although Chinese economy is unstable, their industrial force looks strong. *85*

Lecture

경제가 불안하다 economy is unstable

기업의 기세 business spirit

무섭다 overflow

무서운 기세 mighty force

➜ '무섭다'는 '기세가 넘쳐흐른다'의 의미이므로 'overflow'를 사용한다.

중국 경제가 불안해도(중국경제가 불안하지만) despite 또는 although를 사용한다.

Model Sentence

Although Chinese economy is not stable, their business spirit is overflowing.

18

환투기세력 먹잇감 된
검은 튤립 '홍콩달러'

Words

환투기(환율차익을 노린 달러 보유) investment, predator

먹잇감(희생양) victim, target

검은 튤립(홍콩달러: 현실에 존재하지 않는 귀한 투기의 상징)
black tulip

Phrases

환투기 세력 predator power

먹잇감이 되다 being target

Writing practice

Hong Kong dollar, the black tulip, <u>has become that meant to</u>
<u>victim of</u> predator. *70*

➡ 한글 의미에 맞추어 문장을 간결하게 쓴다.

Correction

Hong Kong dollar, the black tulip, has fallen prey to predator. *95*

Lecture

환투기 foreign-exchange speculation

세력 force

먹잇감 prey

홍콩달러 Hong Kong dollar

➡ 육식동물의 먹잇감 prey

➡ 초식동물의 먹잇감 fodder

먹이로 하다 feed on

➡ 개구리는 곤충을 먹이로 한다 Frogs feed on insect.

먹잇감이 되다 fall to prey for

Model Sentence

Hong Kong dollar, the black tulip, fell to prey for the force of foreign-exchange speculation.

19

바오치(保七 7% 성장) 실패한 중국…
최악은 안 왔다

Words

바오치(保七 7% 성장) 7% growth

실패 fail to

최악 worst

Phrases

안 왔다(아직 오지 않았다) have yet to come

Writing practice

China failed to keep 7% growth, but it has yet to reach its worst.

95

Lecture

바오치 7% 성장 Baoqi 7% growth rate

실패하다 short of

바오치 7% 성장 실패한 중국 China short of Baoqi 7% growth

최악은 안 왔다 the worst has not come. 또는 China failed in maintaining it Baoqi 7%.

Model Sentence

In the China short of its Baoqi 7% growth, the worst has not yet come.

20

법률시장 개방 압박 수위 높이는 4개국
미국·영국·호주·EU

Words

법률시장 law market

개방 open

압박 수위 press level

EU(유럽연합) European Union

Phrases

법률시장 개방 open of law market

압박 수위를 높이다 increase the level of pressure

Writing practice

There are 4 countries such as the U.S., Britain, Australia and EU
to raise their press levels. ✕

➡ 주어를 there로 시작하면서 전달하려는 의미가 불투명해졌다.

Correction

Four countries such as the U.S., Britain, Australia and EU, are
increasing their level of pressure to open our law market. *90*

Lecture

법률시장 legal market

개방 opening

압박 수위 level of pressure

시장 개방을 요구하다 demand an open market

법률시장 개방을 요구하다 demand an open legal market

높이다 increase, raise

Model Sentence

Four countries, the U.S., Britain, Australia and EU, are increasing their pressure level to demand an open legal market.

21 | 영국은 우울증 약 처방하기 전 독서를 권하죠

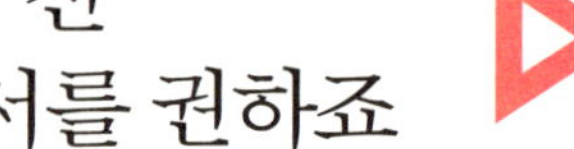

Words

우울증 depression

처방 prescription

독서 reading book

권하다 recommend

Phrases

약 처방 medicine prescript

독서를 권하다 recommend reading book

Writing practice

The British tends to recommend reading books <u>ahead</u> medicine prescription <u>on</u> depression. 80

> ➡ ahead: in or toward the front, 앞쪽으로, 전방

> ➡ prescribe on보다 prescribe for depression 형태로 더 자주 쓴다.

Correction

The British tends to recommend reading books before prescribing medicine for depression. 90

Lecture

우울증 depression

약 처방 medicine prescription

권하다 advise, suggest

독서를 권하다 advise patient to read book

추천하다 recommend

➡ He recommended this dictionary to me. 그가 이 사전을 추천했다.

Model Sentence

In the U.K, doctors advise their patients to read books before getting medicine for depression prescribed.

22

대만 대선에 따른 양안 관계 변화에 주목한다

Words

대선 presidential election

양안(兩岸: 타이완 해협을 두고 분단된 두 중국) both sides, Taiwan and China

관계 relationship, 변화 change, shift, 주목 eye, look to

Phrases

양안 관계 relationship between Taiwan and China

변화에 주목하다 eye on shift

Writing practice

We need to eye on shift of relationship <u>both sides</u> through Taiwan presidential election. *80*

> ➤ both sides 앞에 between이 필요하다.

Correction

We need to pay attention to the shift of relationship between both sides through Taiwan presidential election. *85*

Lecture

대만 대선 Taiwan presidential election

양안 Taiwan and China,

관계변화 change of relation

주목하다 get attention

Model Sentence

The change in bilateral relations between Taiwan and China is getting attention.

23

대북 제재 국면에…
북한 노동자 더 보내달라는
중국 기업들

Words

제재 sanctions

국면 state, situation

노동자 labor, worker

Phrases

대북 제재 sanctions against North Korea

더 보내달라는 (요구) ask for sending more

Writing practice

Under the situation of imposing sanctions against North Korea, Chinese companies have asked for <u>sending</u> more labors from the country. 90

➜ sending이 없어도 의미에 지장이 없으므로 생략하면 문장이 더 간단해진다.

Correction

Under the situation of imposing sanctions against North Korea, Chinese companies have asked for more labors from the country.

93

Lecture

대북 제재 국면에 in the time when sanctions against is being urged

중국기업들 enterprises in China

북한 노동자를 더 보내달라고 요청하다 ask for more workers from North Korea

Model Sentence

In the time when sanctions is being urged, Chinses enterprises want more workers from North Korea.

24

아베 "한국은 전략적 이익 공유하는 가장 중요한 이웃"

Words

아베 (일본 총리) Shinzo Abe

전략 strategy

이익 profit, interest

공유 share

이웃 neighbor

Phrases

전략적 이익을 공유하다 share with strategic interests

Writing practice

Shinzo Abe said that Korea is the most important neighbor country <u>sharing with strategic interests</u>. *92*

➡ share something with someone: share 다음에 공유할 대상이 바로 온다.

Correction

Shinzo Abe said that Korea is the most important neighbor country sharing the strategic interests (with Korea). *95*

Lecture

전략적 이익 strategic interest

공유하다 share

가장 중요한 이웃 the most important neighbor

중요하다 important, significant, crucial

중요하지 않다 little importance

Model Sentence

Japanese Prime Mister, Abe, said that Korea is the most important neighbor sharing the strategic interest.

25

케리,
오늘 중국과 대북 제재 담판 '세컨더리 보이콧'으로 압박할 듯

Words

케리(미국 국무부 장관) John Kerry

담판 discuss, negotiation, conference

세컨더리 보이콧(제재국과 거래하는 제3국 역시 제재를 가하는 전략) secondary boycott

압박 push, stress, strain

Writing practice

Today, the secretary of the United States, John Kerry is likely to push secondary boycott at a conference <u>of sanctions</u> with China against North Korea. *90*

　➡ 전달하려는 의미를 명확하게 표현한다.

Correction

Today, the secretary of the United States, John Kerry is likely to push secondary boycott at a conference with China to impose sanctions against North Korea. *95*

Lecture

존 케리 미국 국무장관 John Kerry

중국과 대북제재 담판 negotiate with China for sanctions against North Korea

"세컨더리 보이콧"으로 압박할 듯 likely to press China with "secondary boycott"

압박하다 press someone for something

누구에게 무엇을 하라고 압박하다 press someone for doing something

➜ 은행이 대출금을 상환하라고 압박하고 있다. The bank is pressing them for repayment of the loan.

Model Sentence

The U.S. secretary of the State would negotiate with China to impose sanctions against North Korea, and would likely to press China with "secondary boycott".

part   03   정치 핫이슈

Politics Hot Issue

01 의원 선출,
스마트폰 살 때만큼 고민하나요

Words

의원 lawmaker

선출하다 elect, vote, choice

고민하다 worry, care, cautious

Phrases

의원 선출 vote for lawmaker

스마트폰 살 때 when you buy a smart-phone

Writing practice

Would you pay attention <u>to vote</u> for lawmaker as much as buying a smart-phone? 85

➡ 이 문장에서 to는 전치사이므로 vote가 아닌 voting이 온다.

Correction

Would you mind voting for lawmaker as much when you buy a smart-phone? 95

Lecture

의원선출, 투표하다 vote for representative

신경 쓰다, 고민하다 pay attention to

의원을 선출할 때 신경 쓰다 They pay attention to voting for representative.

> ➜ '살피다, 신경 쓰다'의 의미로 동사 mind를 사용할 수 있다.

Model Sentence

Voting for your representative, do you mind it as much when you buy your smart-phone?

'백세인생' 로고송 사용료 5억 비싸다고 전해라~

Words

백세인생 100 year life

로고송 logo song

사용료 fare, fee, using fee

비싸다 expensive

전해라 say

Phrases

백세인생 로고송 the logo song for 100 year life

비싸다고 전해라 say that it is expensive

Writing practice

Please, <u>give</u> saying that 500 million won is expensive using fee for the 100 year life as a logo song. *80*

➡ 이 문장에서 동사 give는 불필요하다.

Correction

Please, say that 500 million won to use the 100 year life as a logo song is too expensive. *85*

Lecture

백세인생 100 years life 'logo song'

사용료 fee to use

비싸다고 전해라 send words that it is expensive

Five hundred million won is charged for royalty fee for 'the hundred years old life logo song.'

➜ is charged for에서 charged를 생략하고 is for만 사용하면 문장이 더 간단해진다.

Model Sentence

Put it that five hundred million won to use logo song of the hundred year life is too expensive.

언제까지 정당은 인물에 의존할 것인가

Words

언제까지 by when

정당 political party

인물 figure, person, man, character

의존하다 depend, rely

Phrases

인물에 의존하다 rely on figure

Writing practice

<u>When</u> many political parties rely on their figures <u>by</u>. *80*

> ➜ by 대신에 until이 의미를 더욱 분명하게 한다.

Correction

Until when would political parties rely on their figures? *90*

Lecture

언제까지 how long

> ➔ '언제까지'의 의미는 until when이지만 이 문장의 의미는 '정당은 그들의 정치적 인물에 얼마나 더 오랫동안 의존해야 하는가?'에 더 가깝다.

정당 political parties

인물에 의존하다 rely on their figures.

> ➔ '의존해야 하는가'를 is to rely on으로 사용할 수 있다.

Model Sentence

How longer are political parties to rely on their figures?

04 | 쟁점 법안 대승적 타결로 나라 살려야

Words

쟁점 problem, issue, controversial

법안 bill(통과되지 않은), proposal(제안), law(통과된 법)

대승적 (포괄적 견지) broad view

타결 reach an agreement, 살려야 recover

Phrases

쟁점 법안 the issued bill

대승적 타결 reach an agreement in a broad view

나라를 살리다 to recover the country

Writing practice

It has to <u>recover</u> the country as reaching an agreement in a broad view. *80*

> ➔ 한글 의미에 좀 더 가까운 표현을 찾는다.

> ➔ recover: 회복, 복구

Correction

It has to save the country by reaching an agreement in a broad view. *90*

Lecture

쟁점 on discussion

법안 bill

대승적 타결 reach a consensus

대승적 합의 consensus general agreement

➔ There was consensus among House representative. 미 하원에서 전체적

인 합의가 있었다.

나라를 살리다 save a country

Model Sentence

It is important to reach a consensus to save a country.

05

정부의 폴크스바겐 환경오염 대처에 문제 있다.

Words

정부 government

폴크스바겐(독일 프리미엄 자동차 브랜드) Volkswagen

환경오염 environmental pollution

대처 treat, response, deal with, handle, tackle

Phrases

문제가 있다 have a problem

Writing practice

There is a problem decisively for government to handle <u>on</u> Volkswagen's environmental pollution. *80*

➜ 불필요한 전치사는 생략한다.

Correction

There is a problem decisively for government to handle Volkswagen's environmental pollution. *85*

정치 핫이슈 Politics Hot Issue

Lecture

문제가 있다, 문제에 부딪혔다 is facing a problem

폴크스바겐 환경오염 air pollution by Volkswagen

대처하다 cope with

→ '대처하다'의 경우 deal with를 사용할 수 있지만, cope with something은 deal with보다 successfully with a difficult situation의 의미를 포함한다. 즉 '성공적으로 어려운 일을 잘 처리하다'의 의미이다.

Model Sentence

Government is facing a problem to cope with air pollution by Volkswagen.

06

국민 분노케 하는
장관 후보 자녀들의 '금수저' 특혜

Words

국민 people, public, national, nation, citizen

분노 rage, anger

장관 secretary, minister, head, chief

후보 nominee

금수저 gold spoon in mouth

특혜 special favor, privilege, preference

Phrases

금수저 특혜 special favor for the group of gold spoon in mouth

Writing practice

The special <u>favor on</u> children of some nominees of minister makes people to rage. 80

➡ favor on 대신에 favor for를 사용하는 것이 더 좋은 표현이다.

Correction

The special favor for children of ministerial nominees, 'gold spoon' privilege makes people rage. 90

Lecture

금수저 gold spoon

특혜 privilege

장관후보 ministerial nominee

분노케 하다(분노하게 만들다) anger, make a person angry

장관 후보 자녀들의 금수저 특혜는 국민을 분노하게 만든다.

Model Sentence

1. 'Gold spoon' privilege to children of ministerial nominees angers people.

2. People are angered by 'gold spoon' privilege to children of ministerial nominees.

07

저출산 극복 첫 단추는 청년 주거문제 해결이다

Words

저출산 low birth rate

극복하다 overcome, get over, cope with

첫 단추 first button

청년 young generation

주거문제 housing problem, residence, dwelling, abode

해결하다 solve, resolve, settle

Phrases

저출산 극복 overcome low birth rate

Writing practice

The first button to cope with low birth rate is <u>settlement</u> for solving young housing problem. 80

> ➜ 정확한 단어를 사용해야 한다.

> ➜ settlement: a formal agreement 합의, 정착의 의미

Correction

The first button to cope with low birth rate is solution to solving problem housing for the youth. 90

Lecture

저출산 low birth rate

극복 overcome

첫 단추 first step

청년 주거문제 housing problem

주거문제 해결이다 way to solve the housing problem for the youth

Model Sentence

A first step to overcome the low birth rate is a way to solve the housing problem for the youth.

08

노동개혁 정부지침,
필요하지만 신중하길

Words

노동개혁 labor reformation

정부지침 government guideline

신중하다 cautious, careful, discreet

Writing practice

Some kind of guidelines from government is necessary to labor reformation, but it needs cautious moving. *75*

➡ reformation: 교정, 감화, 개심   reform: 개혁, 쇄신

Correction

Some kind of government guidelines is necessary to labor reform, but it needs to be cautious. *85*

Lecture

노동개혁 labor reform

정부지침 Government guideline

필요하지만 신중하길(필요하다, 그러나 신중히 다루어져야 한다)
necessary, but must be well handled.

➜ '신중한'을 위해 deliberate을 사용할 수 있다. 하지만 이 헤드라인에서는 '처리
가 잘 되어야 한다'는 의미로, 'must be well handled'이 더 가깝다.

Model Sentence

Government guideline for labor reform is necessary, but careful
approach is desired?

09 | 저유가와 원화 약세, 더 이상 득이 아니다

Words

저유가 low oil price

원화 Korean currency

약세 weakening, be weaken, become weak, be lessened

더 이상 any more

득(유익) gain, profit, advantage

Phrases

더 이상 득이 아니다 no more advantage

Writing practice

It may be said to be no more advantages are low oil price and weakening Korean currency. *75*

➜ 주어가 정확하면 의미전달이 분명해진다.

Correction

Low oil price and weak won may not be good any more. *95*

Lecture

저유가 low price oil

원화 약세 weak won currency, devalued won currency

득이 되다 gain

더 이상 득이 되지 않는다 is not gaining any more

Model Sentence

Low price oil and weak won is not gaining any more.

10 | 최고책임자 빼고 실무자 징계 요구한 메르스 감사

핫이슈 영작 Hot Issue English Composition

Words

최고책임자 chief, head, executive

빼다 miss, take out, get out, exclude

실무자 be in charge, charge, responsibility

징계 discipline, punish, penalize, reprimand

요구하다 ask for

메르스(중동호흡기증후군, MERS) Middle East Respiratory Syndrome, 감사 audit, inspection

Writing practice

The inspection on MERS <u>is that</u> asks for punishing just its charger but excluding the head. *75*

> ➜ is that을 생략하면 문장이 더 간단해진다.

> ➜ charger 배터리 충전기

Correction

The inspection on MERS asked for punishing just its officials, excluding the head. *90*

Lecture

최고책임자를 빼다 count the highest officials in charge out

실무자 hands on officials

징계하다 punish

메르스 감사 the inspection of MERS

징계를 요구하다 ask for punishing

메르스 감사는 최고책임자를 제외한 실무진 징계 요구했다.

Model Sentence

The inspection of the MERS asked for punishing the working
level, counting out the official in charge.

'월남 패망론' 담화,
41년 전 아버지 데자뷔

Words

월남(베트남) Vietnam

패망(붕괴) defeat, rout, ruin, collapse

담화(연설) speech, announce, address

데자뷔(프랑스어. 진부한 것, 기시: 접하는 것을 경험한 듯 여기는 착각) déjà vu

Phrases

패망론 (사건, 이야기) the event of Vietnam collapse

Writing practice

The address on the event of Vietnam collapse was déjà vu of her father 41 years ago. ✕

➡ 월남 패망론에 관한 연설이 아니라 "연설 속에 언급된 월남 패망론"을 명확하게 표현한다.

Correction

The Vietnam collapse remarked in her address was déjà vu of her father 41 years ago. *95*

Lecture

월남 패망론 Vietnam defeat logic

담화 statement

데자뷔 déjà vu, already seen(기시감)

> ➔ 불어 **déjà vu**의 의미는 'the illusion or feeling that you have already seen something that is actually happening for the first time(현재 진행되고 있는 강력한 감정이 과거에 이미 경험한 것처럼 느껴지는 현상)'이다.

Model Sentence

She used her rhetoric of 'Vietnam collapse logic' in her address, déjà vu reminding her father 41 years ago.

국회 5개월째 태업…
0%대 주저앉은 경제

Words

국회 National Assemble

태업(태만) a work stoppage, neglect, idly, default

주저앉다 fall down, drop, lapse (~상태로 빠지다)

경제 economy

Phrases

0%대로 주저앉다 fall down to 0% level

Writing practice

The state of National Assemble default consecutive 5 months leads to fall down to economy on 0% level. *80*

→ 보다 간단히 표현하면 더 좋은 문장이 된다.

Correction

The state of National Assemble default for 5 months brought our economy down to 0% growth. *85*

Lecture

태업 slowdown

국회 national assembly

0%대로 주저 않다 fail down to 0%

5개월째 five months of national assembly slowdown

국회 5개월째 태업 때문에 경제가 0%로 주저앉았다.

Model Sentence

Due to five months of slowdown of the National Assembly, our economy fell down to 0% growth.

13 | 학대의 대물림,
이대로 방치할 것인가

Words

학대 assault, abuse, mistreat, cruelty, harassment, wrong

대물림 hand down, transmit, leave

방치하다 leave alone, neglect, lay aside, let it goes

Phrases

이대로 (그대로) as it is, like that, intact

Writing practice

How we the handing down of mistreat neglect like that. 70

➡ 주어를 잘 선택하면 좋은 문장을 만들 수 있다.

Correction

Handing down assault on their children should not be neglected as it is. 90

Lecture

학대의 대물림 child abuse is being passed down to children
이대로 방치되어야 할 것인가? Shall it be left untouched this way?
학대가 대물림 되고 있다. 이대로 방치되어야 할 것인가?

Model Sentence

Child abuse passed down to child; shall it be left this way?

14

아동학대 신고한 교사·학생, 법으로 보호한다

Words

아동학대 child abuse

신고 report, inform

교사 teacher, educator

법 law

보호하다 protect, take care, give sanctuary

Writing practice

Both <u>educators</u> and students <u>who informs</u> kind of child cruelty are to protect by law. *75*

→ 될 수 있는 대로 문장을 간단하게 쓴다.

→ and/or 의미를 좀 더 정확하게 사용한다.

Correction

Teachers or students reporting child abuse are to be protected by law. *90*

Lecture

신고한 교사 teacher reporting

법으로 보호하다 protect by the law

아동학대 금지법을 입법화하다 legislate against the child abuse

아동학대 금지법이 입법화했다. They legislated against the child abuse.

Model Sentence

Teachers or students reporting child abuse are to be protected by the law.

15

대북 제재 머뭇대는 중국엔 네 갈래 시선 있다

Words

대북 제재 sanctions against North Korea

머뭇대다(망설이다) hesitate, waver, hold back

갈래(나뉘다, 부분, 다르다) faction, branch, differ, part

시선 sight, view, eyes, looking, idea

Phrases

네 갈래 four different parts

Writing practice

China <u>is observed</u> that it is holding back sanctions against North Korea due to have four parts solutions. 75

> observe는 'to make a comment about something'의 뜻으로 누군가의 의
> 견을 말할 때 사용한다. 따라서 여기에서 중국의 현재 상황을 기술하는 데는
> 알맞지 않다.

Correction

China, hesitant to impose sanctions against North Korea, is being seen in four ways. 95

Lecture

대북 제재 sanctions against North Korea

머뭇대다(머뭇거리다) hesitate

네 갈래 시선 four lines of eye

대북 제재 머뭇거리는 중국은 네 갈래 시선을 맞이하고 있다.

Model Sentence

China hesitant to impose sanctions against North Korea is meeting four lines of eye.

16

롯데,
일본 계열사 허위 자료 제출,
공정위, 내주 제재 절차 밟기로

Words

롯데그룹(한국인이 일본에서 설립한 기업) Lotte Group

일본 계열사 Japan affiliate, units, subsidiaries, arm

허위 자료 fake report, false information, fabricated data

공정위(공정거래 위원회) Fair Trade Commission

제재 punishment, 절차 procedure, process, steps, proceeding

밟다 step forward, move, undergo

Writing practice

<u>With</u> one of affiliate in Japan of Lotte Group had submitted false
data, Fair Trade Commission here steps forward to punish on the
group next week. *80*

> ➡ 간단하게 표현할수록 좋은 문장에 가까워진다.

Correction

One of Japanese Lotte Group affiliates submitted false data, and
the Fair Trade Commission here will take step to punish the
group next week. *95*

Lecture

롯데 계열사 Lotte affiliate

허위 자료 false data

공정위 Fair Trade Commission

제재 절차 sanction procedure

밟기로 하다 decide to take sanction measure

Model Sentence

1. One of Lotte affiliates was found to file its false data, and the Fair Trade Commission decided to work on sanction measure against it.

2. One of Lotte affiliates was found to file its false data, and the Fair Trade Commission decided to take a measure for sanction against the group unit.

17

우물에 빠진 정치
새 판 짜서 희망 보여줘야

Words

우물 well

정치 politics

새 판 new strategy, new plan, new vision

희망 vision, hope, wish, desire, aspiration

Phrases

우물에 빠지다 fall into well

Writing practice

The politics being fallen into well <u>is forged</u> new vision and then show people hope. *75*

➡ '보여줘야 한다'는 한글 의미를 명확하게 표현한다.

Correction

The politics being fallen into well must forge new frame, and then show people its hope. *90*

Lecture

우물에 빠진 정치 politics sunk into a well, politics dipped in well
새 판을 짜다 form a new situation
희망을 보여주다 show hope, give hope

Model Sentence

Politics dipped in a well, need to form new situation, giving hope.

18

국민 요구는 먹고 사는 문제

Words

국민 public, people

요구 demand, asking, require, call

먹고 사는 livelihood

문제 issue

Phrases

국민 요구 people demand

Writing practice

The only demand <u>to people</u> is the issue living eating. *75*

→ to people을 by people로 표현한다. 전치사에 따라 의미가 크게 달라진다는
점을 유의하자.

Correction

The only demand by people is the issue of livelihood. *90*

Lecture

국민은 요구하다 people wants

먹고 사는 문제 make a living

먹고 사는 문제(민생, 생계) livelihood

해결하다 solve a problem

국민은 먹고 사는 문제를 해결해주길 요구한다.

Model Sentence

People want their livelihood to be solved.

19 | 정치 비상사태 풀려면
대통령과 국회 지도부 만나야

Words

정치 politics

비상사태 the emergency situation

풀다 life, release

대통령 the president

국회 National Assembly

지도부 leader group, the board of leaders

만나야 meet, talk

Writing practice

<u>In order to resolve</u> the emergency situation on politics, the president needs to sit down with the leaders of lawmakers. *85*

> 될 수 있는 대로 문장을 간단하게 쓴다.

Correction

To untie the emergency situation on politics, the president needs to sit down with the leaders of lawmakers. *95*

Lecture

정치 비상사태 political emergency situation

풀다(엉킨 것을 풀다) untangle

국회지도부 leaders of National Assembly

만나다 get together

Model Sentence

President and leaders of National Assembly must be arranged to get together to have the political emergency situation untangled.

총선서 다 살아오세요

Words

총선(국회의원 선거) general election, parliamentary election

다 (회원 모두) the member of the party

살아오다(승리하다, 표를 획득하다) get a victory, get a grip

Phrases

다 살아오다 all of the member bring grand win

Writing practice

Make a landslide victory and <u>return</u> at its headquarter vividly. 85

> ➔ 여기에서 '살아오다'는 의미는 '본부로 무사히 돌아오라'는 것이 아니라 '살아남다', '이기다'의 의미다.

Correction

Make a landslide victory, and come back vividly. 95

Lecture

총선 general election

다 살아오세요 win and come again

총선에서 승리하세요 don't fail in the general election. 또는 do not lose the general election.

Model Sentence

1. Come on, you everybody, don't lose the general election.
2. Win it and come back again.

part   04   경제 핫이슈

Business   Hot   Issue

객실 부대시설 줄인 특2급 호텔, 용품 다르지만 품격은 그대로

Words

객실 room, compartment, 부대시설 facility

특2급 호텔 four star hotel

용품 supplies, goods, utensil

품격 grace, rank, grade

Phrases

부대시설 줄인 curtailed facility

용품 다르지만 differ from utensil grade though

Writing practice

Four star hotels curtailed their facilities of rooms, but it keeps their <u>grace</u> as usual despite differing from supplies. *80*

➡ 보다 적합한 단어를 사용하면 뜻이 분명해 진다.

➡ 편의시설: amenity

➡ grace는 은총이고 dignity는 품위다.

Correction

Four star hotels curtail rooms and amenity, but it keeps their dignities as usual despite differing from supplies. *90*

Lecture

객실 부대시설 rooms and amenities

줄인 less

용품 supplies

품격은 그대로 same dignity, same level of dignity

객실 부대시설을 줄인 특2급 호텔이 다른 용품을 제공하지만 품격은 같은 수준을 유지하고 있다.

Model Sentence

The special second grade hotel with less rooms and amenities keeps same level of dignities, though different supplies.

02 편의점 전성시대
백화점·대형마트는 한숨 쉬는데 성장률 나 홀로 연 8%대

Words

편의점 convenience store

전성시대 the heyday, the golden age

대형마트 large store, mart, supermarket

성장률 growth rate, 나 홀로 only

Phrases

한숨 쉬다(낙담하다) sigh, disappoint, depress

Writing practice

Many convenience stores only marked 8% growth rate last year <u>because</u> enjoying its heyday, while department stores and supermarkets are depressed. *80*

➜ 어법에 맞게 쓰면 더 좋은 문장이 된다.

Correction

Many convenience stores only marked 8% growth rate last year, enjoying its heyday alone, while department stores and supermarkets sigh. *95*

Lecture

편의점 convenience store

전성시대 golden age

한숨 쉬다 sigh

성장률 나 홀로 연 80%대 enjoy their annual growth rate 80%

나 홀로 alone

백화점 ~ 쉬는데

→ 접속사 'while'을 사용한다

Model Sentence

Convenience stores in their golden ages enjoy their annual growth rate 80% or more alone, while department store and supermarkets sigh.

단돈 1,000원…
커피 정글에 뛰어든 편의점

Words

단돈 just money

정글 jungle

편의점 convenience store

뛰어들다 join, rush, run, jump into

Writing practice

The convenience stores jump into jungle of coffee business, enticing by priced just 1000 won. *90*

Lecture

단돈 1000원 single piece money 1,000 won

커피정글 coffee jungle

뛰어들다 run into

편의점이 단돈 1,000원짜리 커피를 무기로 커피정글에 뛰어들었다

Model Sentence

Convenience stores run into coffee jungles serving coffee for only 1,000 won.

하반기 올랐던 중국 증시,
산소호흡기 뗄 시점에 경련

Words

하반기 the second half of the year

증시 stock market

산소호흡기 oxygen mask, aided breath tool, breathing machine

경련 spasm, jerk, convulsion

Phrases

호흡기를 뗄 시점에 at the time when the breathing machine is tried to detach

Writing practice

Although China market had risen in the second half of last year, it got spasm at the time when the aided breathing machine was tried to detach. *80*

➡ '경련이 일다'는 동사 convulse를 쓴다.

Correction

Although Chinese market had risen in the second half of last year, its situation has turned to convulse at the time when the aided breathing machine was removed. *90*

Lecture

하반기 second half

주식이 오르다 shares rise

산소호흡기 oxygen mask

호흡기를 떼다 remove oxygen mask

산소호흡기를 뗄 시점에 경련을 일으키다 convulse at the point of removing the oxygen mask

Model Sentence

하반기에 올랐던 중국 증시가 산소호흡기를 뗄 무렵에 경련을 일으켰다.

Chinese stocks that rose in the second half, convulsed at the time of the oxygen mask being removed.

한미약품
전 직원 4,000만 원씩 (1인당 평균) '주식 선물'

Words

한미약품 Hanmi pharmaceutical company

전 직원 whole employees

1인당 평균 at average per pay roller

Writing practice

Hanmi Pharmaceutical Company gave all of employees <u>for</u> a stock gift valued 40 million won at average each. *85*

➜ 여기에서 for는 불필요하다.

Correction

Hanmi Pharmaceutical Company gave all of its employees a stock gift valued at 40 million won each on the average. *95*

Lecture

한미약품 Hanmi pharmaceutical

전 직원 staff as whole

주식선물 stock as gift

4,000만 원씩 주식선물 gift of stock valued at 40 million won (average each one)

Model Sentence

The Hanmi pharmaceutical gave his staff as whole gift of stock valued at 40 million won each.

Words

포근한 warm

지역 경기 reginal economy

꽁꽁(얼다) tightly frozen

곳감 a dried persimmon

생산 produce

급감하다 decrease rapidly, be sharply reduced

Writing practice

Since this winter is warm generally but reginal economy is frozen <u>hardly</u>, the amount of produce of dried persimmon has been reduced sharply. ✕

➜ 부사 hardly(almost not)로 인해 정반대의 문장이 된다.

Correction

Since this winter is generally warm but reginal economy is frozen, the amount of produce of dried persimmon has dropped sharply by 40%. *95*

Lecture

포근한 겨울 warm winter

지역 경기 '꽁꽁' local zones is in recession

곶감 생산 dried persimmons produce

40% 급감 drop sharply down to 40%

포근한 겨울인데도 지역 경기는 불황을 맞고 곶감 생산이 40%로 급감했다.

Model Sentence

With warm winter, local countries are in recession, and dried persimmons produce dropped sharply down by 40%.

기업 기밀 많이 접하는데…
일부 회계사 일탈 감시는 허술

Words

기업 corporate

기밀 secrecy information

접하다 close accept, get

회계사 (공인) a treasurer, an accountant

일탈하다 depart, deviate (빗나가다)

감시하다 oversee, supervise, monitor

허술하다 careless, poor looking, plain, shabby, negligent

Writing practice

Despite a lot of information of corporal secrets close around here, it is plain monitoring against accountants. *80*

➡ 의미가 좀 더 분명하게 드러나도록 표현한다.

Correction

A lot of information of corporal secrets is close around here; it is because of careless monitoring accountants' deviation. *90*

Lecture

기업 기밀을 많이 접하는데(기밀이 많이 노출되는데) exposed to many top secret

일부 회계사 some of public accountants

일탈 감시 watching deviation

허술하다 lenient short of

많은 기업 기밀이 노출되고 있는 원인은 일부 회계사들의 일탈행위에 대한 감시가 소홀하기 때문이다.

Model Sentence

Being exposed to many of top secrets is because of being short of watching public accountants' deviation.

시절이 수상하니
금값이 꿈틀꿈틀

Words

시절 time, season

수상하다 suspicious, doubtful, questionable

금값 gold price

꿈틀꿈틀하다(불안정하다) wriggle, squirm, unstable

Phrases

시절이 수상하다 its season is questionable on stability

금값이 꿈틀꿈틀 the price of gold is starting to move

Writing practice

<u>Now that</u> the seasonal market is doubtful on stability, gold price is starting to move by steps. *85*

➡ now that: ～이기 때문에

Correction

The stability of the seasonal market is doubtful on; gold price is starting to move up. *90*

핫이슈 영작 Hot Issue English Composition

Lecture

시절 time

수상하다 suspect

꿈틀꿈틀 (나아가다) worm

물가가 천천히 오르다 worm up 또는 move up

수상한(불안정한) 시절을 맞이해서 금값이 천천히 올라갈 준비를 하고 있다는 의미

Model Sentence

Suspecting time, gold price gets ready to move up.

"FTA 시대, '승리'의 키워드로 만리장성 넘어라"

Words

FTA(자유무역협정) Free Trade Agreement

시대 era

키워드 key word

만리장성 The great wall

넘다 overcome, jump over, go beyond, go over

Phrases

승리의 키워드 victory has to become a key word.

만리장성을 넘다 go over the limit of the great wall

Writing practice

We need to overcome the limit of China <u>which is called as</u> the great wall, putting our effort <u>to</u> a key word of victory. *80*

➡ put on 전치사 사용에 주의한다.

Correction

We need to overcome the Great Wall of China, putting our effort on a key word of victory. *90*

Lecture

FTA 시대 FTA time

'승리'의 키워드 'victory' key word

만리장성 the Great Wall

넘다 go through

만리장성을 넘다 go through the Great Wall. Go beyond the Great Wall

FTA 시대를 맞이하여 승리의 키워드로 만리장성을 뛰어넘자.

Model Sentence

Coming across FTA globalization, let's jump over the Great Wall.

10 | 낮아진 관세, 빨라진 배송…
K뷰티 대륙 방방곡곡 달군다

Words

관세 tariff, 배송 delivery

K뷰티(한국 화장품 산업) global beauty industry of Korean

대륙 China continent

방방곡곡 across all direction

달구다 busy from their asking

Phrases

낮아진 관세 tariff lower

빨라진 배송 delivery faster

Writing practice

Global K-beauty industry <u>make hit across land of China</u> through both lower tariff and faster delivery system. *85*

➡ 필요하지 않은 어휘는 생략하여 간단히 한다.

Correction

Global K-beauty industry is catching on all over China with both lower tariff and faster delivery system. *95*

Lecture

낮아진 관세 Customs taxes are lowered. Lowered customs taxes

빨라진 배송 quick delivery

K뷰티 K-Beauty

달구다 heat, catch on

낮아진 관세와 빨라진 배송으로 K뷰티가 중국 방방곡곡을 달구고 있다.

Model Sentence

With lowered customs taxes and quick delivery system, K-Beauty is catching on all over China.

11 한 해에 3조원 이상 '팍팍'
기업 재단 사회 공헌 '쑥쑥'

Words

팍팍 spend a lot

기업 재단 company foundation

사회 공헌 social contribution

쑥쑥 jump up, hop

Phrases

한 해에 3조 이상 more than 3 trillion a year

Writing practice

It spends money for more than 3 trillion won a year from some company's foundation so that delivers contributions a lot. *80*

➡ 핫이슈의 의미를 명확하게 파악하여 주어를 선정한다.

Correction

Enterprise foundation, which spends more than 3 trillion won a year, is rushing to make contribution to society. *100*

Lecture

기업 재단 enterprise foundations

한해 3조 원 3 trillion won

한해 32조 원 이상 '팍팍' Spend more than 3 trillion won in an abrupt way

기업 재단 사회 공헌 '쑥쑥' enterprise foundations are moving their contribution to society upward

Model Sentence

Spend more than 3 trillion won in an abrupt way; enterprise foundations are moving their contribution to society upward.

12 | "원금 걱정 마세요" 믿었는데…
땅 치는 ELS 투자자들

Words

원금 the principal, capital

파생결합주식(ELS) Equity Linked Securities

투자자 investor

Phrases

원금 걱정 마세요 don't worry about the principal

땅을 치다(후회하다) regretful, flowing of regret

Writing practice

Although some ELS investors believed in commercials such as, don't worry about your money invested, they are now sorry what's happening. 95

Lecture

'"원금 걱정 마세요" 믿었는데'이 문장의 주어는 ELS 투자자들이다.
즉 '원금 걱정 마세요'를 말한 사람들은 ELS이다.
위 문장을 다음과 같이 바꿀 수 있다.

➡ ELS가 투자자들에게 '원금 걱정 마세요'라고 했을 때 투자자들은 믿었다. 하지만 지금은 몹시 후회하고 있다.

원금 걱정 마세요 Don't be worried about your principal money.
투자자들은 땅을 치고 있다(투자자들은 몹시 후회하고 있다)
lament 동사를 이용한다.

Model Sentence

ELS investor said they believed when ELS told them not to be worried about the principal money. Now they lament their investment.

13

"경상흑자 확대는
　　성장 잠재력 훼손 신호"
　기업 내부 비축자금 투자로 연결해야

Words

경상흑자 a surplus of revenues

잠재력 potential power

훼손 damage, undermine, destroy

비축자금 saving funds, capital

Phrases

경상흑자 확대 increase of revenues

성장 잠재력 훼손 신호 a sign of damage of potential growth power

자금 투자로 연결하다 lead to invest funds

Writing practice

Because increasing of revenues implies a sign of damage of potential growth, it needs to lead to invest. *90*

Lecture

경상흑자 흑자 surplus current account balance

확대되다 run up

성장 잠재력 훼손 damage potential growth

비축자금 fund in reserve

투자로 연결해야 하다 must be linked to investment

경상수지 확대는 성장 잠재력 훼손 신호이기 때문에, 이것은 투자로 연결해야 한다.

Model Sentence

Running up surplus current account balance is a sign damaging potential growth, to avoid the loss, the enterprise funds in reserve must be linked to further investment.

14

늦기 전에 막차 타세요…
사라지는 알짜 카드들

Words

막차 final train, final chance

사라지다 disappear, go away, out, vanish

알짜 essence, the best, the cream

타세요(잡으세요) catch, take, ride

Phrases

막차를 타다 ride a final train

Writing practice

Let's get a chance before <u>missing</u> that the best cards will face to vanish. *80*

   ➡ 한글 표현을 보다 영어답게 구체적으로 표현한다.

Correction

Let's get a final chance before the best cards being vanished. *95*

Lecture

늦기 전에 막차 타세요 Aboard the last train before you are late.

사라지는 going out

알짜카드 creamy cards

늦기 전에 마지막 기회를 잡으세요. 사라지는 알짜 카드를 잡으세요.

Model Sentence

Catch the last opportunity before benefit-cards have vanished.

15

분양시장은 식을 줄 모르고,
기존주택엔 찬바람 불고

Words

(주택) 분양시장 housing sale

식다 cool, get cold, reduce(줄다, 약해지다)

기존주택 existing house, traditional house, current house

찬바람 a cold wind

Phrases

분양시장은 식을 줄 모르고 housing sale isn't getting down

기존주택엔 찬바람 불고 current house is blowing a cold wind

Writing practice

Housing sale isn't getting down and existing houses are <u>blowing a cold wind</u>. *85*

   ➡ 한글 문장은 영어에 가깝게 바꾸어서 표현한다.

Correction

Housing sale isn't getting down, while housing market is rare in dealing. *90*

Lecture

분양시장 condominium market

열기가 식을 줄 모르다 fever never cool down

기존 주택 existing houses

찬바람이 불다, 경기가 불황이다 head toward, recession

> ➜ '식을 줄 모르다'는 thrive로, '찬바람이 불다'는 head toward 또는 slow down 으로 바꾸어 사용한다.

Model Sentence

Condominium market is still thriving and the existing houses are slowing down.

16

해외 인재 모여드는 '아시아 실리콘밸리' 만들자

Words

해외 foreign countries, overseas, abroad

인재 a man of ability, a man of talent, a competent person

모이다 gather, rush, come in haste

Phrases

아시아 실리콘밸리 Asian Silicon Valley

해외 인재 foreign competent person

Writing practice

Let us make here as an Asian Silicon Valley <u>which is gathered by</u> competent person from abroad. *75*

➡ 문장을 어법에 맞추면 좋은 문장이 되고 물과 같이 부드럽게 흐른다.

Correction

Let us make here an Asian Silicon Valley where competent persons gather from abroad. *90*

경제 핫이슈 Business Hot Issue

Lecture

해외 인재 oversea good brains

모여들다 gather

아시아 실리콘밸리 Asian Silicon Valley

지금은 해외 인재들이 모여드는 아시아 실리콘밸리를 만들 시기다.

➜ 패턴 'it is time that' 을 이용한다.

Model Sentence

It is time that we build an Asian Silicon Valley, where a number of good brains gather around from oversea.

17

주택시장 혼란 자극하는 통계 착시

Words

주택시장 housing market

혼란 confusion, mess

자극 stimulate, promote, spur

통계 statistic

착시 confuse, optical illusion, mistake

Phrases

주택시장 혼란 housing market confusion

통계 착시 statistic illusion

Writing practice

Statistic illusion stimulates to confuse _of_ housing market. *90*

➡ 동사 confuse는 of를 필요로 하지 않는다.

Correction

Statistic illusion stimulates to confuse housing market. *95*

Lecture

주택시장 housing market

혼란을 자극하다 put something or someone in confusion

통계착시 statistic illusion

Model Sentence

Statistic illusion puts the housing market in confusion.

18

스피드 경영, 한국 문화 담은 상품이 중국서도 통한다

Words

스피드 speed

황급한 rapid

신속, 즉각 promptness

경영 management, conduct

문화 culture

상품 product, goods

통하다 through, worked, pass

Phrases

문화 담은 상품 product showing their culture

Writing practice

Speedy management and <u>showy cultural goods</u> serve in Korea, so does China. 70

→ 영어에 가까운 표현일수록 좋은 영어작문이 된다.

Correction

Speedy management and goods of Korean culture are doing good in Korea, so does China. 80

Lecture

스피드 경영 speed management

문화 담은 상품 goods of culture

통하다 get along

'스피드 경영'과 '한국 문화 담은 상품'은 동격이다 speed management goods of Korean culture

통하다, 사이가 좋다 get along, go through

Model Sentence

Speed management and goods of Korean culture are going well through China.

19

초심 잃지 않으려고
한라산 50번 뛰어오르며
느림보 극복

Words

초심 one's original intention, first willing

한라산 Mt. Hallasan

뛰어오르다 rush climbing, jump up

느림보 a dawdler, a laggard

Phrases

잃지 않다 in order not to lose his original intention

Writing practice

He overcame his laggardness by climbing Mt. Hallasan 50 times a day in order not to lose his original intention. *90*

Correction

He overcame his laggardness by climbing Mr. Hallasan even 50 times a day not to lose his original intention. *95*

Lecture

초심 first resolution

초심 잃지 않으려고 not for forget my first intention

뛰어오르다(무대 위를 뛰어오르다) jump onto the stage

산을 뛰어오르다 Go up mountain

한라산을 50번 뛰어오르다 have gone up mountain (Mt) Halla fifty times

느림보를 극복하다 overcome being lazy

➡ 느림보는 dawdle이라고도 한다.

초심을 잃지 않기 위해 한라산을 50번 뛰어오르며 게으름을 극복했다.

Model Sentence

Not to forget my first resolution, I overcame being lazy by going up mountain Halla fifty times.

20

여성의 성공은 운이 아니다

Words

성공 success

운 lucky, fortunes

Phrases

여성의 성공 success of woman

운이 아니다 it is not fortunes.

Writing practice

It is hard to say <u>what</u> woman got a success is just fortunes. *85*

> ➜ what을 that으로 수정한다.

Correction

It is hard to say that women's success is attributed to their lucky.

95

Lecture

여성의 성공 women's success

운이 아니다 not good luck

여성의 성공은 운이 좋아서 성공했다고 말할 수 없다.

Model Sentence

1. We don't put women's success down to good luck.

2. Women's success is not just good luck.

21

대형 손보사도 자동차 보험료 인상 시동

Words

대형 big size, large scale, grand structure, massive volume

손보사(손해보험회사) an insurance company

자동차 보험료 motor insurance

시동 start

Phrases

보험료 인상 raise insurance

Writing practice

<u>Also</u> some of top insurance companies start to raise their motor <u>insurance rate.</u> *90*

Correction

Some of top insurance companies also start to raise their motor insurance premium rate. *95*

Lecture

대형 손보사 large damage insurance

자동차 보험 car insurance premium

인상 시동 be about to increase, willing to raise

보험업에 종사하다 works in insurance

보험에 들다 insure

> ➜ 보험에 들었어? Are you insured?

Model Sentence

Large damage insurance companies are about to raise premium for car.

22

우주선 만드는 탄소섬유로 자동차 무게 400kg 줄인다

Words

우주선 spacecraft, space shuttle, spaceship

탄소섬유 carbon fiber

줄이다 cut, reduce

Phrases

자동차 무게 the weight of car

Writing practice

The car weighs down <u>to 400kg</u> with some kind of carbon fiber using spaceship. *80*

- ➡ down to 대신에 down by로 쓴다.(down to 400kg: 400kg까지 줄인다는 의미)
- ➡ used for spaceship 우주선에 사용하는

Correction

The car weighs down by 400kg with carbon fiber used for spaceship. *90*

Lecture

우주선 spaceship

우주선 만드는 탄소섬유 carbon fiber used to make spaceship

➡ 우주선 만드는 탄소섬유로 전치사 with를 사용한다.

With the carbon fiber used to make spaceship

자동차 무게 automobile's weight

줄이다 reduce

Model Sentence

We can reduce the automobile weight by 400kg with the use of carbon fiber used to make spaceship.

연매출 100억 원
외국계 로펌 첫 등장

Words

연매출 yearly revenue

외국계 foreign

로펌 law firm

첫, 처음 first time

등장하다 come up on stage, entrance, introduce, appearance

Writing practice

It is first time <u>for</u> foreign law firm <u>to</u> come up on stage with 10 billion won revenue yearly. *80*

> ➡ It is~ that 패턴을 사용한다. It is ~ for ~ to 패턴은 이 문장에서 적절하지 않다.

Correction

It is first time that one of foreign law firms comes up earning 10 billion won in revenue. *95*

Lecture

연매출 annual sales

외국계 로펌 foreign law firm

연매출 100억을 올리다 turn over ten billions won for annual revenue

한 외국계 로펌이 처음으로 연매출 100억 원을 올렸다.

Model Sentence

A foreign law firm has turned over ten billion won in the annual revenue for the first time.

샤오미 저가폰의 비밀
'특허 무단 사용'

Words

샤오미(중국 전자제품 제조사) Xiaomi

저가폰 low priced smart phone

비밀 secret

특허 patent

무단 사용 illegal use without notice

Phrases

특허 무단 사용 illegal patent use, patent using illegally

Writing practice

<u>It is unfolded</u> the secret of low priced Xiaomi small phone as using the patent illegally. 80

➜ 한글 의미에 가깝게 표현할수록 좋은 영어 작문이 된다. 주어 선택에 따라 의미가 더욱 분명해진다.

Correction

The secret of Xiaomi's low price is to use others' patents illegally. 95

Lecture

샤오미 Xiaomi

저가폰 low cost phone

무단 사용 illegal use, unauthorized use of patents

저가폰의 비밀 secret of Xiaomi low cost phone

특허 무단 사용에 있다 lay in unauthorized use of patents

샤오미 저가폰의 비밀은 특허 무단 사용에 있다.

Model Sentence

The secret of Xiaomi low cost phone lies in the illegal use of patents.

'금융 성과주의 도입' 더는 눈치 안 본다

Words

금융 finance

성과주의 meritocratic

도입 introduce, bring in

눈치 be aware, sense, be conscious

Phrases

금융 성과주의 financial meritocratic

Writing practice

With <u>bring</u> in financial <u>meritocratic</u> system, there is no more being conscious others. 75

→ meritocratic system는 이익이 되는 제도이고 성과주의는 performance system 이다.

→ 전치사 다음에는 명사나 동명사가 와야 하므로 with bring이 아니라 with bringing이 되어야 한다.

Correction

Finance companies don't mind anymore introducing its performance system. 95

Lecture

금융 financial companies

성과주의 도입 performance system

도입하다 introduce

더 이상 눈치 안 본다 steal glance no more, not steal glances anymore

Model Sentence

Finance companies introduce performance system, so their employees don't need to steal glances at others any more.

26

경험도 자격도 없는
'불량멘토'가 '스타트업 생태계' 망친다

Words

경험 experience

자격 eligible, deserve, qualification

불량멘토 poor mentor

스타트업 start-up

생태계 ecosystem

망치다 spoil, damage, ruin

Phrases

경험도 자격도 없다 neither experience nor eligibility

Writing practice

Poor <u>mentor who is</u> neither experienced nor eligible ruins start-up's ecosystem. *85*

> ➜ who 앞에 콤마가 오는 것이 좋다.

Correction

Poor mentor, who have neither experience nor eligibility, ruins start-up's ecosystem. *95*

Lecture

경험도 자격도 없는 no experience and no qualification

불량멘토 faulty (poor) mentor

생태계 ecology

스타트업 start-up

망치다 botch (carry out a task badly, or carelessly)

> ➜ 일 또는 프로젝트를 망치다 He was criticized to botch the job. 그는 그 일을 망쳤다고 비난 받았다.

Model Sentence

Poor mentors, who have neither experience nor any qualification, are botching the ecology system of start-ups.

27

은행원들은 임금피크제보다 희망퇴직 선택

Words

은행원 a bank clerk, a bank worker

임금피크제 wage peak system

희망퇴직 voluntary retirement

선택 option, choice

Writing practice

Some bank workers opted voluntary retirement <u>than</u> wage peak system. *75*

➡ 여기서는 비교가 아니라 '대신'이라는 의미다. than보다 instead of 또는 rather than이 적합하다.

➡ opt보다는 choose를 사용하면 더 좋다.

Correction

Some bank workers choose voluntary retirement instead of wage peak system. *95*

Lecture

은행원 teller

임금피크제 salary workshare program

희망퇴직 early retirement

정년퇴직 regular retirement

퇴직금 severance pay

→ He spent much of his retirement travelling. 그는 퇴직 후 대부분을 여행하면서 시간을 보냈다.

은퇴 retirement (He announced his retirement from international football.)

선택하다 choose

Model Sentence

1. Tellers choose desired retirement rather than the salary workshare program.

2. Tellers choose early retirement rather than the peak salary system.

28

경기 따로, 물가 따로

Words

경기 economy

물가 price

따로 apart, divide, split

별개 separately

Writing practice

The price is <u>apart from</u> its economy separately. *70*

→ 영어를 정밀하게 표현할수록 한글 의미에 가까워진다.

→ apart from은 besides ～이외에도 라는 의미다.

Correction

Economy and price are separate. *80*

Lecture

경기 business

물가 prices

따로 separately

> ➜ separately는 not together(함께하지 않는, 따로 따로)라는 의미다.

Model Sentence

Business and prices are going separately.

29 | 한국 바이오 투자 '10대 제약' 합쳐도 노바티스의 6%

Words

바이오 (생명) biology, biography, bio-

투자 investment

제약 pharmaceutical, pharmacy

노바티스(스위스 다국적 제약회사) Novartis

Writing practice

The combined top ten pharmacies for Korean Bio investment come under only 6% of Novartis. *80*

→ The combined Bio investment of Korean top ten pharmacies. 이런 순서로 쓸 수 있다.

Correction

The Korean ten Bio pharmacies investment combined make up for 6% of Novartis. *90*

Lecture

~에 투자하다 invest money in something

~에 해당되다 make up

노바티스의 6%에 해당된다 make up 6% of the one (that) made by Novatis

"한국 바이오 투자 '10대 제약' 합쳐도"라는 한글 문장을 "바이오에 투자한 한국 10대 제약사를 합쳐도"로 재구성해본다.

The amount combined, of which the largest 10 pharmaceutical companies in Korea invested in biotech,

Model Sentence

The amount combined, of which the largest 10 pharmaceutical companies in Korea invested in biotech industry, make up just 6% of that of Novatis.

37년 제재 해제
이란 특수 120조

Words

제재 sanctions

해제 lift

특수 special, unique

Writing practice

It is a special opportunity <u>for its valued</u> 120 trillion won on lifting sanctions of Iran in 37 years. *70*

➡ 정확한 주어를 찾으면 표현력이 강해진다.

Correction

It is a special opportunity that Korea will gain value of 120 trillion won from lifting sanctions on Iran in 37 years. *80*

Lecture

37년 만에 제재 해제 lifting of sanctions on Iran in 37 years

특수 120조를 누리다 enjoy the increased demand for 120 trillion won

한국기업 Korean companies.

특수를 누리다 anticipate the increased demand

Model Sentence

Companies are anticipating the increased demand valued at 120 trillion won since lifting of sanctions on Iran in 37 years.

part   05   문화 핫이슈

Culture Hot Issue

드론으로 네팔 오지 마을에 의약품을 전달한다고

Words

드론(무인승 비행기) drone

오지(도시에서 멀리 떨어진 시골) outback, hinterland

의약품 medicine

전달 deliver

Phrases

드론으로 by drone

네팔 오지 마을에 at the outback in Nepal

Writing practice

It is surprised that you deliver medicine at the outback in Nepal by drone. *70*

➡ It is a surprise 표현이 맞다.

➡ at the outback이 아니고 to the outback이다.

Correction

It is a surprise that they deliver medicine to the outback in Nepal by drone. *90*

Lecture

드론으로 by drone

네팔오지 마을에 to the remoted villages in Nepal

의약품 medicines

전달하다 deliver

이 문장의 주어는 they로 한다.

그들의 말에 따르면 I wonder they say

그들이 한다고 I wonder they would

Model Sentence

I wonder they would deliver medicines to the remoted villages in
Nepal.

 | # 3040 CEO들이 말하는 최고의 유산

Words

CEO (최고 경영자, 대표이사) Chief Executive Officer
유산 (후대에 이어지는 역사적 문물) legacy, heritage
3040(30대, 40대 사람들) 30s and 40s demography

Phrases

CEO들이 말하는 CEO's saying
최고의 유산 the most legacy

Writing practice

It is the most legacy of CEO 30s and 40s saying. *70*

➡ 어법에 맞는 순서로 쓴다.

Correction

It is the best legacy CEOs in 30s and 40s are saying of. *95*
It is the best legacy that CEOs in 30s and 40s are saying of.

Lecture

최고의 paramount

유산 heritage

Model Sentence

3040 CEO takes them as one of the paramount heritages, the paramount heritage 2030 leaders would say of.

03 냉동실서도 세균 살아요, 한 달 지나면 아까워도 버리세요

Words

냉동실 freezer

세균 germ, bacteria

아깝다(유감이다) dear, valuable, precious, regrettable, pitiful

버리다 throw away, disposal

Phrases

냉동실에서도 살다 the germ is living even in a freezer

아까워도 버리다 throw away it pitiful though

Writing practice

Since the germ is living in a freezer, <u>things even valuable</u> have to <u>dispose</u> at the time when it is passed over one month. *70*

   → to dispose는 to be disposed가 맞다.

Correction

As the germ is living in a freezer, let foods disposed when one month passes, even valuable though. *85*

Lecture

냉동실 freezer

세균 germ

살다 survive

한 달이 지나면 once the food goes, Past one month

버리다 throw away

세균은 냉동실에서도 삽니다. 음식물이 한 달이 지나면 버리세요.

Model Sentence

Germ may survive in the freezer. Once it goes past one month,
throw it away.

서해 갯굴은 남해 굴보다 작지만
맛과 향이 진하고
식감이 쫄깃쫄깃하다

Words

갯굴 oyster

맛 taste, flavor, savor, 향 flavor

식감 texture, be tough, 쫄깃쫄깃하다 chewy

Phrases

맛과 향에서 in taste and flavor

식감이 쫄깃쫄깃하다 texture is chewy

Writing practice

The oyster from West Sea is smaller than the South Sea, not only better taste and flavor, but also chewy texture. 75

➡ 문장을 좀 더 명료하게 다듬는다.

➡ '진하다'의 의미로 deep를 쓴다.

➡ one from the South Sea가 바른 표현이다.

Correction

Despite oyster from West Sea is smaller than one from the South Sea, it has not only better taste and flavor but also chewy texture. 80

234

Lecture

서해 갯굴은 남해 굴보다 작지만 yellow sea oyster is smaller-
sized than
맛과 향이 진하다 taste and aromatic are dense
식감이 쫄깃쫄깃하다 mouthfeel is dense and chewy

Model Sentence

Yellow sea oyster is smaller-sized than southern sea one, but it is
more tasty and aromatic, with chewier mouthfeel.

스타워즈 셔츠,
도라에몽 립 틴트…
"재밌고 추억 떠올라 선호"

Words

도라에몽(일본만화 캐릭터 파란 고양이 로봇) Doraemon

립 틴트 lip tint

재미있다 fun, interesting, exciting

추억 memory

선호 preference

Phrases

추억이 떠오르다 come up a memory

Writing practice

The shirt drawing Star War's image and the lip tint imaging
Doraemon are <u>popular</u>, because of funny memory from them. *70*

Correction

The shirt drawing Star War's image or a lip tint imaging
Doraemon is preferred because of funny memory from them. *85*

Lecture

스타워즈 셔츠 star wars shirts

도라에몽 립 틴트 Doraemon lip tint

재미있다 very interesting

추억이 떠오르다 recall some memories

Model Sentence

Star wars shirts and Doraemon Lip tint are interesting and recalling memories.

06 얼굴처럼 매끈·촉촉하게, 손발도 팩으로 가꾸세요

Words

매끈하다 slippery, smooth, oily

촉촉하다 moist, wet

팩(얼굴관리 마스크) facial mask pack

가꾸다(관리하다) care, take care of

Phrases

얼굴처럼 like your face

손발을 팩으로 가꾸다 take care of hands and feet with exclusive pack

Writing practice

Please <u>care as</u> your hands and feet with exclusive pack <u>much as</u> moist your face. 75

> ➡ care as 대신 take care of를 사용한다.

> ➡ 전치사 어법에 주의를 기울인다.

Correction

Please take care of your hands and feet with exclusive pack like your slick and moisty face. 95

238

Lecture

얼굴처럼 매끈하게 slick like face is

촉촉하게 moisty

매끈하고 촉촉한 얼굴처럼 like slick and moisty face

가꾸다 take care of

손발도 팩으로 가꾸세요. 손발을 팩으로 가꾸세요.

매끈하고 촉촉한 얼굴처럼 손발을 가꾸세요.

Model Sentence

Like your slick and moisty face, take care of your hands and feet.

Words

교통 traffic

생활 life

편의 convenience, facilities, advantage

미래 in the future

갖추다 be ready, have

복층형 오피스텔(복층 구조) duplex type Officetel (office+hotel)

Writing practice

There are Officetels <u>being ready</u> high valued advantage of convenience, traffic, and future for life. *80*

➡ '시설을 갖추다'의 의미로 complete with를 사용한다.

Correction

Duplex type Officetels complete with advantage of convenience, traffic, and future value. *90*

Lecture

교통·생활편의 convenience of transportation and living,

미래가치 future value

다 갖추다 complete with

복층형 오피스텔 duplex officetels complete with

Model Sentence

Duplex Officetels complete with the convenience of transportation and future value.

08 | 그린벨트 해제 기대감 부풀고
주변 개발 바람 불고

Words

그린벨트 green belt

해제 lift, release

기대 expectation

부풀다 expand, get big, be buoyant, be inflated

주변 around, surroundings, near, periphery, edge, vicinity

개발 develop

Phrases

기대감이 부풀다 hope is getting big

개발 바람이 불다 tending of developing blow

Writing practice

Hopes are getting big for lifting Green Belt and making wind at peripheral development. *70*

➜ 영어문장은 한글 감각과 차이가 있음을 이해한다.

Correction

The Green Belt has getting bigger hopes for expectancy of lifting; the peripheral region is breezing as its development. *85*

Lecture

그린벨트 해제 Greenbelts release

기대감 부풀고 expectation billows

주변지역 circumjacent area

개발 바람 불고 wind of development blows

Model Sentence

Expectation of Greenbelt release billows with wind of development on the circumjacent area.

09

동네 빵집으로 13년 버틴 힘은 정성과 좋은 재료

Words

동네 빵집 town bakery

정성 effort, sincerity, devotion

재료 (원료) ingredient, material, stuff

Phrases

버틴 힘 power to survive

Writing practice

Only devotion and good materials make <u>power</u> of standing as a humble town bakery for 13 years. *70*

➔ 한글 문장 감각으로 영어를 표현하면 의미가 밀어진다.

Correction

The power to survive for 13 years as a town bakery is just humble devotion and good materials. *85*

Lecture

동네 빵집 neighborhood bakery

13년을 버티다 survive 13 years

정성과 좋은 재료 sincerity and good stuff

버틴 힘 power something to do

동네 빵집으로 13년간 버틸 수 있는 힘을 준 것은 성실과 좋은 재료였다.

Model Sentence

Sincerity and good stuff gave power for the neighborhood bakery to survive 13 years.

10

통독 후 동독 학생들이 배우던 과목 폐지 대혼란…

Words

통독 German unification

동독 East Germany

과목 subject

폐지 abolish

대혼란 confusion, mess

Phrases

배우던 과목 subject which they learned

Writing practice

After German <u>was unified, closing</u> subjects being learned cause great confusion. *80*

➡ 폐지는 closing보다 abolition이 더 적합하다.

Correction

After German unification, the abolition of the subjects they learned in East caused a great confusion. *90*

Lecture

통독 후 after the German's unification

동독 학생들이 배우던 과목 폐지 abolition of curriculums that East Germany students learned

대혼란 a great shambles

통독 후 동독 학생들이 배우던 과목 폐지는 대 혼란으로 이어졌다.

Model Sentence

Since Germany unification, the abolition of curriculums that East Germany students led to a great shambles.

11

매일 영화(2시간짜리)
9,200만 편 왕래 '데이터 고속도' ··· 주파수 더 필요해

Words

왕래 traffic

고속도 high speed

주파수 frequency

Phrases

주파수 더 필요해 need more frequency

Writing practice

<u>The frequency needs highway of data</u> because of the traffics of 2 hour long 92 million films every day. *70*

➡ '2시간 왕래'기 이니라 '9200만 편의 왕래'임을 보다 명확히 한다.

➡ 주어는 '데이터 고속도'가 되어야 한다.

Correction

The highway of data needs further frequency because of the traffics of (2 hour running per movie) 92 million films every day. *85*

Lecture

매일 영화 everyday movies (2 hours running)

9,200만 편 왕래 '데이터 고속도' data high way speed, in which 9200 million movies travel

주파수 frequency

더 필요하다 require more

Model Sentence

"Data high way" speed making 92 million movies (2 hours running) travel every day requires further frequency.

12

"방학 땐 하고 싶은 것 해라"…
숙제 없앤 교장선생님

핫이슈 영작 Hot Issue English Composition

Words

방학 vacation

숙제 homework

교장선생님 headmaster

Phrases

하고 싶은 것을 하다 do what you want

숙제를 없애다 homework is got rid of

Writing practice

<u>The president of school</u> got rid of homework on their vacation, saying what students want do. *80*

> ➜ Do what you want 네가 하고 싶은 것을 해라.

> ➜ president of school는 대학 총장을 말하는 경우가 많다.

Correction

The headmaster got rid of homework on their vacation, saying do what you want. *90*

Lecture

하고 싶은 것을 하다 do what you want to
방학 때 as school breaks up
교장선생님 school headmaster
숙제를 없애다 get rid of homework
"방학 땐 하고 싶은 것을 하라"고 하면서 교장선생님은 숙제를 없애버렸다.

Model Sentence

The school headmaster said, "do what you want to as school breaks up," and he has got rid of homework.

13

“세월은 피부를 주름지게 하지만,
열정을 저버리는 것은
영혼을 주름지게 한다”

핫이슈 영작 Hot Issue English Composition

Words

세월 times

주름 winkle

열정 passion

저버리다 avoid, ignore

영혼 sole, sprit

Phrases

피부를 주름지게 하다 make winkles on skin

열정을 저버리다 ignore passion

Writing practice

While times make winkles on face, what ignores passion makes winkle on their sole. 93

Lecture

세월 time

피부를 주름지게 하다 make skin wrinkle

열정을 저버리다 abandon passion

영혼을 주름지게 하다 crease on spirit

세월은 피부를 주름지게 한다, 한편 열정을 저버리는 것은 영혼을 주름지게 한다.

> ➡ 두 구문을 and로 연결한다.

> ➡ General Douglas MacArthur had written "Years may wrinkle the skin, but to give up interest wrinkles the soul."

Model Sentence

Time makes skin wrinkle, and giving up with passion makes crease on spirit.

14

정확하고 빠른 '로봇 명의'…
전립선암 수술 80% 맡아

Words

정확 accuracy

명의 noted doctor

전립선암 prostate cancer

수술 operation, surgery

Phrases

수술을 맡다 operate surgery

Writing practice

Robot doctor <u>which is accurate and fast</u>, operates 80% of surgeries on prostate cancer. 85

→ which is를 생략하면 더 간단한 문장이 된다.

Correction

Accurate and fast robot doctor operates 80% of surgeries on prostate cancer. 95

Lecture

정확하고 빠른 '로봇 명의' accurate and fast "robot doctor"
한글 의미를 재구성한다.
정확하고 빠른 '로봇 명의'가 전립선암 수술의 80%를 맡는다.

Model Sentence

An accurate and fast ‛robot doctor operates on 80% of prostate cancers.

핫이슈 영작 Hot Issue English Composition

15 피부 건조해지면 간질간질…
때 밀지 말고 보습제 바르세요

Words

피부 skin

건조 dry

간질간질 feel creepy

밀다(때를 밀다) scrub

보습제 supplementary supplies

바르다 put, apply, correct

Writing practice

Where it feels creepy on dried skin, doesn't scrub but apply supplementary. 80

➡ where 내신에 if를 사용하면 좋은 문장으로 바뀐다.

Correction

If it feels creepy on dried skin doesn't scrub but apply supplementary. 95

Lecture

피부가 건조해지면 if skin is dried

보습제 humectants

바르다 apply를 사용한다

때 밀지 말고(오염을 미는 것 대신에) instead of pushing filth

Model Sentence

피부가 건조해서 간질간질할 경우 때를 밀지 말고 보습제를 바르세요.

If it feels like being creepy on dried skin, don't scrub, but apply humectants.

16

맨손체조로 체온 올린 뒤 스트레칭하면 운동 효과 만점이죠

Words

맨손체조 free gymnastics, free standing exercises

체온 body temperature

스트레칭 stretching

효과 effect

만점 perfect

Phrases

체온을 올린 뒤 after raising body temperature

운동 효과 exercise effect

Writing practice

When stretching is followed to raise body temperature by free gymnastics, exercise leads to perfect effect. 95

Lecture

맨손체조 bare gymnastics

체온을 올리다 rise up body temperature

스트레칭을 하다 stretch body

운동효과 workout

만점 cannot be better

맨손체조로 with bare gymnastic

스트레칭하면 효과 만점이죠 If stretching, its workout cannot be better.

Model Sentence

If you do a stretching after rising up your body temperature, its workout cannot be better.

17

부모와의 상호작용이 아이 두뇌 발달의 관건

Words

부모 parents

상호작용 interaction

아이 child, children

두뇌 brain

발달 development

관건 a key point

Phrases

두뇌 발달 brain development

Writing practice

Interaction between child and parents gives good effect on brain development. *95*

Lecture

부모와의 상호작용 interaction with parents

아이 두뇌발달 brains development of kids

관건 key to

Model Sentence

Interaction with parents is a key to brains development for kids.

18

전방 북한군이 흥얼거린 노래
남한 와서 보니 '사랑의 미로'

Words

전방 the front

북한군 (the) North Korea military

흥얼거리다 hum, croon, sing

미로 a maze

Phrases

남한 와서 보니 come to (the) South and find

사랑의 미로 a maze of love

Writing practice

The song that had being hummed by the North Korean soldiers was got to know as "A maze of love" after coming the South. *75*

➡ 영어문장을 간단하게 물이 흐르듯이 표현한다.

➡ 주어가 불분명하다.

Correction

The song hummed by the North Korean soldiers was proved to be "A maze of love" when I came to the South. *95*

Lecture

전방 북한군 North Korean soldiers

흥얼거린 노래 humming song

남한에 와서 보니 finding what it is on coming to South Korea

Model Sentence

North Korean soldiers humming song, having come to South Korea, finding the melody was 'Sarangui miro'(translated 'love maze').

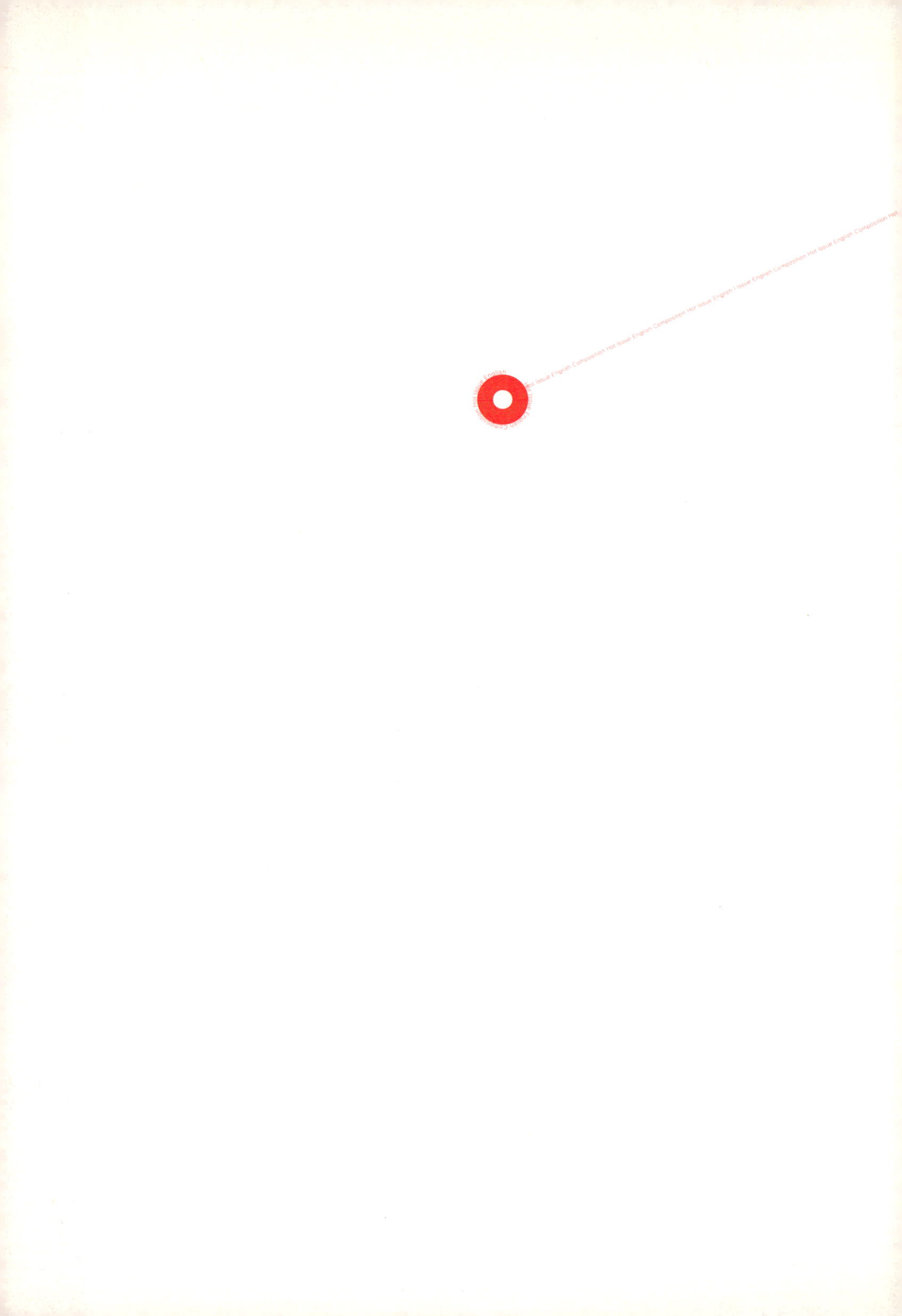
Hot Issue English Composition Hot Issue English Composition Hot Issue English Composition Hot

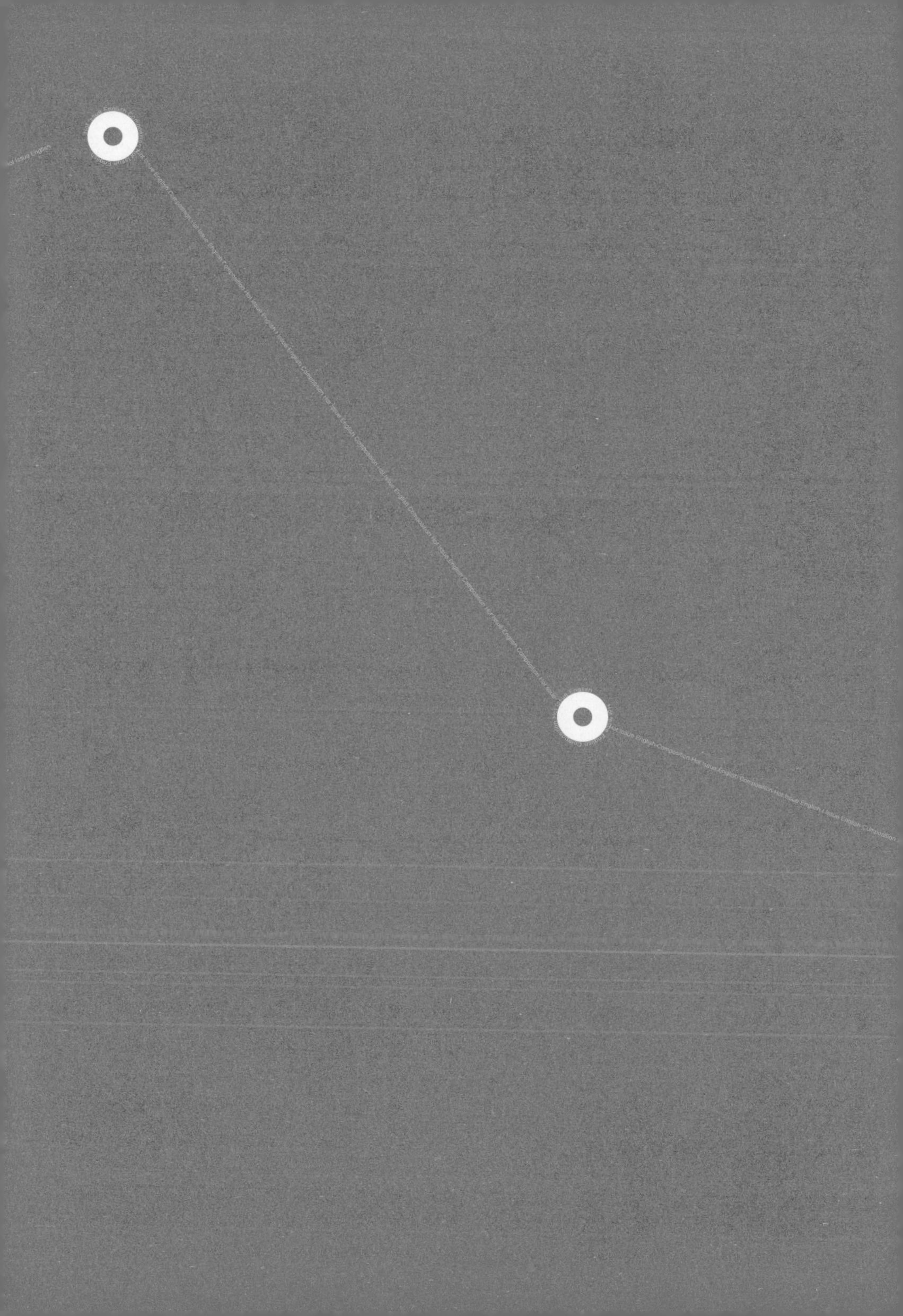

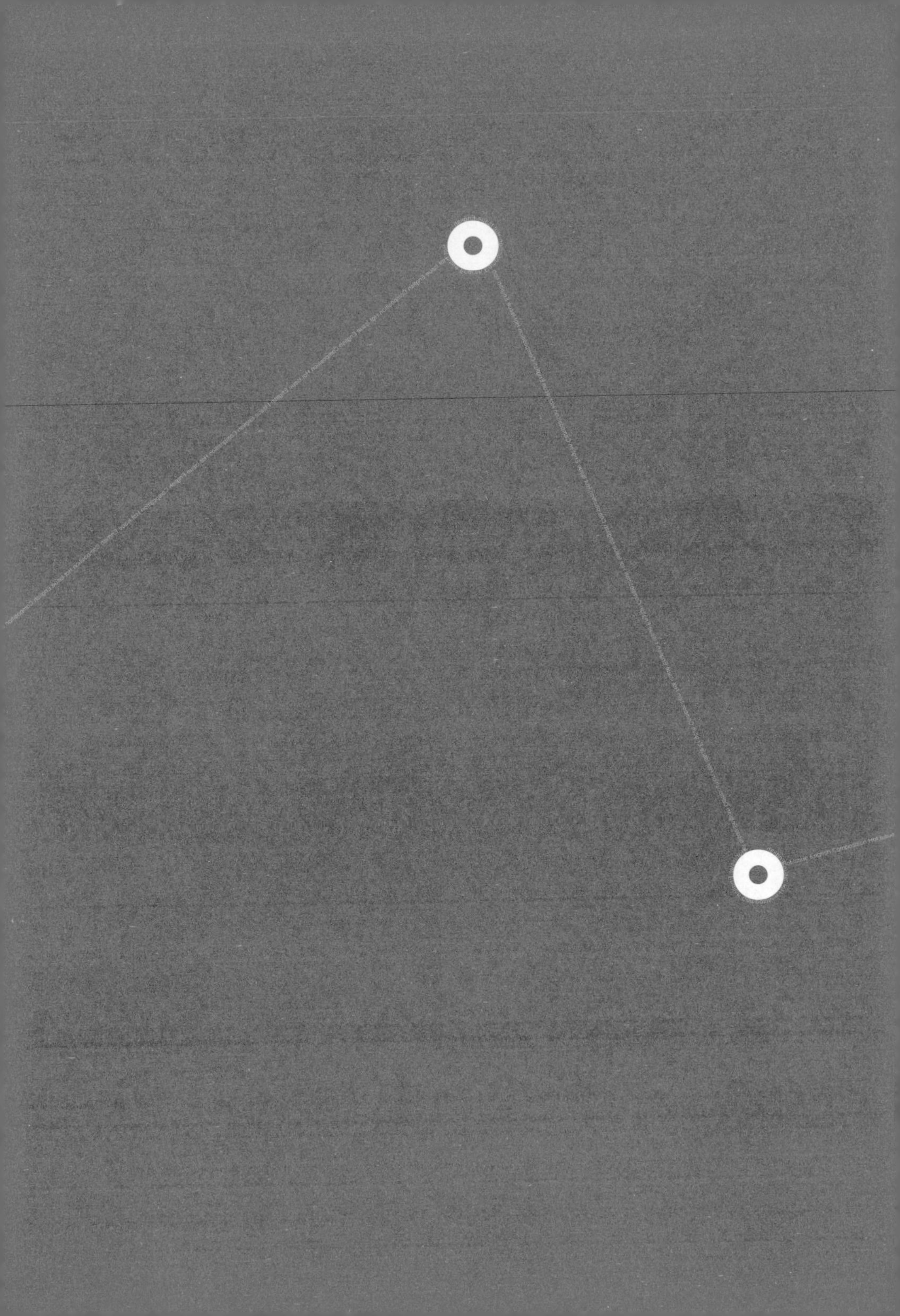